GLOBE
TRAVEL SERIES

CRUISE GUIDE

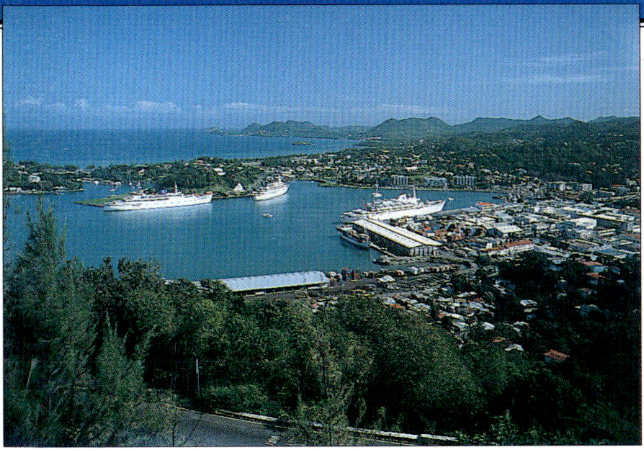

SANDRA BOW

NEW HOLLAND

GLOBETROTTER
TRAVEL SERIES

First edition published in 1998 by
New Holland Publishers (UK) Ltd
London • Cape Town • Sydney • Singapore

10 9 8 7 6 5 4 3 2 1

24 Nutford Place
London W1H 6DQ
United Kingdom

80 McKenzie Street
Cape Town 8001
South Africa

3/2 Aquatic Drive
Frenchs Forest, NSW 2086
Australia

ISBN 1 85368 880 0

Commissioning Editor: Tim Jollands
Editor: Donald Reid
Design and DTP: Behram Kapadia
Cartographer: William Smuts
Reproduction by Modern Age Repro House Limited, Hong Kong
Printed in Hong Kong / China by South China Printing Company (1988) Limited

Front Cover Photographs
Top left: *Two of the* WINDJAMMER BAREFOOT *fleet under sail.* **Top right**: Sun Princess *transiting the Panama Canal.* **Bottom left**: *The riverboat* American Queen *cruising along the Mississippi.* **Bottom right**: *Venice, one of the most popular cruise destinations in the Mediterranean.*
Back Cover Photograph: *CUNARD's mighty flagship, the* Queen Elizabeth 2, *the last of the great liners and guaranteed star billing in New York.*
Title Page Photograph: *Cruise ships lined up in Castries harbour, St Lucia.*

Acknowledgements:
The author wishes to thank the many companies and individuals who have assisted with the research of this publication.

Photographic Credits:
Abercrombie & Kent, 155, 162; **Airtours Cruises**, 72; **Blue Lagoon Cruises**, 47; **CTC Cruise Lines** 42, 66; **Captain Cook Cruises**, 159; **Carnival Cruise Lines**, 12, 22, 40, 54, 75, 76; **Commodore Cruise Line**, 77; **Coral Princess Cruises**, 160; **Crystal Cruises**, 6. 30, 49, 79, 113; **Cunard Line**, back cover, 4, 10, 11, 26, 34, 80, 135, 166; **Delta Queen Steamboat Company**, front cover (bottom left) 68, 149; **Deutsche Seereederei**, 82; **Hapag-Lloyd Cruises**, 19, 86; **Hebridean Island Cruises**, 124, 153; **Holland America Line**, 87, 88; **Maurice Joseph**, 14, 128, 133, 136; **Norma Joseph**, 70, 81, 167, 168; **Jubilee Sailing Trust/Chris Bradley**, 65; **Behram Kapadia**, 164; **Marine Expeditions/Andrew Wenzel**, 69; **Metro Holdings**, 28, 90; **NYK (Nippon Yusen Kaisha) Cruises**, 91; **Norwegian Cruise Line (NCL)**, 92, 109; **Orient Lines**, 93, 127; **Phoenix Reisen**, 95; **Photobank/Adrian Baker**, 154; **Photobank/Jeanetta Baker**, 1, 85; **Photobank/Peter Baker**, 9, 37, 46, 52, 78, 106, 114, 120, 121, 125, 143, 152, 156, 157; **Photobank/Gary Goodwin**, 25; **Princess Cruises**, front cover (top right and bottom right), 7, 13, 17, 29, 33, 40, 53, 62, 96, 111, 116, 118, 165; **P & O Cruises**, 60, 67, 94; **Quark Expeditions**, 161, 163; **Quicksilver Connections**, 134; **Radisson Seven Seas Cruises**, 18, 97; **Donald Reid**, 38, 139; **Royal Caribbean International**, 20, 23, 43, 51, 61, 99; **St Lawrence Cruise Lines**, 151; **Seabourn Cruise Line**, 39, 101, 123; **Spice Island Cruises**, 8, 21, 55, 103; **Star Clippers**, 144; **Strand Voyages**, 138; **Swan Hellenic Cruises**, 105, 131; **Venice Simplon-Orient-Express**, 158; **Whitsunday Adventure Sailing**, 145; **Windjammer Barefoot Cruises**, front cover (bottom left), 45, 56, 59, 141, 146.

CONTENTS

CUNARD

1
Introducing Cruising

Quite simply, cruising has become one of the most popular types of holiday around today. Each year, over five million people take a cruise, and the industry is currently experiencing its greatest ever boom, both in passenger numbers and in the variety of cruises now offered by hundreds of cruise lines based in every part of the globe. While North American itineraries – in particular to the **Caribbean** and **Alaska** – still boast the largest share of the market, traditional cruising areas such as the **Mediterranean** and **Northern Europe** are also expanding, while relatively untapped sectors such as **Southeast Asia** and the **South Pacific** are becoming increasingly popular. If ever there was a way of travelling to make you feel that were truly 'seeing the world', it is cruising.

The key to cruising's popularity is in its **broad appeal**. No longer is it the preserve of a rich elite: while you can still cruise in ultimate luxury, competition is fierce among cruise lines offering **budget deals**, all-inclusive **holiday packages**, **family-oriented cruises** and mind-boggling new **mega-ships** packed with top-grade facilities. Cruising has very successfully broken down barriers of **age**, **class** and **mobility** – a cruise is a particularly attractive option for disabled holidaymakers – and, far from its reputation as a staid and conservative option, now offers exciting opportunities to explore places such as **Antarctica** and the **Amazon**. Alongside these adventures, specialist companies also offer a wealth of unusual and alternative cruises, including windjamming **sailing ships**, 'tramp' **cargo ships** and specialist **explorer cruises**.

The World's Most Exciting Harbour

The most exhilarating way to enter a coastal city for the first time has to be by sea. One of the great rituals of cruise ship passengers leaning on the rail as their ship arrives in or departs a great harbour is to argue long and hard about the merits of various contenders for the title of the World's Most Exciting Harbour. Most lists include the following:

- **Hong Kong**
- **Sydney**
- **Cape Town**
- **Acapulco**
- **Istanbul**
- **New York**
- **Rio de Janeiro**

But there are many more . . .

Opposite: *The world's most famous cruise ship, the* Queen Elizabeth 2, *graces the equally famous New York skyline.*

The Ultimate Address

The Norwegian company ResidenSea intends a new 85,000grt ship due for launch in 1999. Boasting all the amenities that one would expect from an upscale modern vessel, *The World* is no ordinary cruise ship, rather a floating resort housing 280 luxury apartments (yes, apartments!), each costing between US$1.2 million and US$4.2 million.

THE ESSENTIALS OF CRUISING

Cruising aficionados are enthusiastic about the unique experience of taking to the seas, but what is it about going on a cruise that sets it apart from other forms of holiday?

Convenience

On a cruise ship, you may visit several different countries during the course of a holiday, but your 'hotel' always moves with you, so you only need to unpack once. Also, the fact that extensive amenities can usually be found on board means you never have far to go to the nearest shop, restaurant or bar – and at the end of the night you only have to take a few steps to get to your cabin, without having to worry about driving or finding your way back to your hotel or guesthouse.

Your moving hotel is also a **comfortable** and **secure** one, often more so than its shoreside equivalent. You can dismiss fears of having to navigate a myriad of narrow passageways, tiny hatches and wind-swept decks swamped by breaking waves, as modern cruise ships, fitted with elevators and wide corridors, mean that elderly and less-mobile passengers, including wheelchair users, regularly cruise with few problems. Cruise ships also provide a secure environment for children and single holidaymakers – especially females, who might otherwise prefer not to travel alone – and **crime** is virtually nil on cruise ships, so you can wear your sparkling gemstones aboard and rest assured that they will lie safely in a security box whenever you venture ashore.

Below: *Postcards from paradise – cruising is a great way to mix easy-going elegance with exotic destinations.*

Above: *Hotel or high seas? The luxurious atrium on* Sun Princess.

Variety

One of the great assets of cruising is that it allows you to visit several holiday destinations in a relatively short space of time, so if you're not impressed with one particular place it's no big deal – tomorrow you will be somewhere else. There are currently over 1000 different cruise ships – as well as innumerable freighters, sailing yachts and river boats – offering itineraries which, literally, span the globe.

The scope of location offered by cruising is mirrored by the **activities** on offer. The joy of a cruise is that you can do as much – or as little – as you want, and many ships have so many activities packed into the day that you are more likely to be spoilt for choice than bored. The fact that there are so many choices available and so many lines in operation means that competition is fierce and most of the major companies are building ships with increasingly high passenger capacities to allow them to reduce costs and offer still lower fares.

Glamour

Although the industry has changed dramatically since the golden age of the great liners, there is little doubt that glamour and romance still attaches itself to cruising. Not all cruise lines, of course, like to perpetuate the image of dressing for dinner and sipping champagne under the stars, and while some ships are more formal than others, there are plenty offering cruises that are in no way stuffy. Neither is cruising the preserve of older people, with cruise lines reaching out to passengers of all age groups – including honeymooners – and many attracting an increasing number of young families.

The Seasickness Myth

Ships have come a long way since the days of Columbus, and stabilizers are a standard feature of most modern sea-going vessels. This, combined with the fact that many of the more popular routes tend to be in calmer waters, makes seasickness much less likely than many people fear. However, if you're the the sort of person who goes green on your local boating lake, you will want to make sure that *mal de mer* does not spoil your holiday. There are various effective remedies available, while a quick injection from the ship's medical staff shortly after you board should ensure you are fine for the rest of the cruise.

Commonly Asked Cruising Questions (1)

Q: *Where on the ship does the crew sleep?*
A: As a general rule, the Captain, Chief Engineer and various other officers will have cabins near the bridge; senior Hotel officers (such as the Hotel Manager and Cruise Director) may have quarters in passenger areas; and most staff and crew members will have cabins near or below the waterline. Although senior personnel usually have (often spacious) single accommodation, most crew members share cabins for two to four people.

THE CRUISING WORLD

The cruising world reflects many of the current trends in global tourism, with **increased choice** being the primary development. It is now possible to take a cruise to almost any part of the globe, including rivers and lakes as well as the seven seas. Reduced prices, resulting from an increase in the number of ships and their passenger capacities, have made exotic itineraries and extended voyages (such as full world cruises) more accessible. This affordability, combined with the growing consumer demand for far-reaching destinations and different modes of travel, has contributed greatly to the changing face of the cruise industry.

Cruising styles also tend to reflect the interests of the industry's broadening clientele. In the burgeoning Southeast Asian marketplace, for example, shipboard gambling is the predominant attraction. Themed cruises, where the appeal of a voyage is integrated with a common special interest, or cruises with a unique style, such as those by freighter or tall sail ship, also have their niche in the wide world of cruising.

One of the most significant developments in recent years is the increased marketing of cruising as an integral part of a **complete package holiday**, as opposed to a single voyage. Cruises combined with flights, transfers,

Right: *Cocktails and cruising in Indonesia aboard* Bali Sun Dancer.

Above: *Cruise ships lined up in the busy harbour of Charlotte Amalie in the US Virgin Islands.*

stays at land-based hotels and resorts have become a popular vacation choice. Indeed, many major cruise lines have not only joined forces with hotels and holiday resorts, but their ships have come to emulate them. Most of the larger, recently built passenger vessels have all the amenities, comfort and design features associated with deluxe land-based resorts and hotels.

Cruising for **families** is an area of considerable growth, with most of the industry's major players now vying for the family trade, and particularly in popular cruise regions such as the **Caribbean** and **Mediterranean**. But that is not to say that all Caribbean or Greek island-hopping is mainstream. Small specialist lines, charterers and operators also offer a diversity of unusual cruise opportunities aboard a wide range of vessels.

Such diversity is also reflected in cruising's other popular regions – **Alaska**, **coastal Mexico** and the **Baltic** – and developing cruise regions, such as the **South Pacific** and **Indian Ocean**. Often the choices may include vessels indigenous to the region, such as the windjammers of **Maine** or the passenger cargo ships of **Scandinavia**. Yachts, riverboats, schooners, freighters and Arctic ice-breakers combine with regular cruise ships of all shapes, styles and sizes to offer a wealth of choice for every traveller in today's cruising world.

Cruise-Ship Jams

In the more popular ports-of-call around the world yours will almost certainly not be the only ship in town. If you want to get away from it all – and unless you happen to enjoy crowds and inflated prices – steer clear of the following ports in peak season:

- **Charlotte Amalie** (St Thomas)
- **Philipsburg** (St Maarten)
- **San Juan** (Puerto Rico)
- **Nassau** (Bahamas)
- **Miami** and **Fort Lauderdale** (Florida)
- **Juneau** and **Ketchikan** (Alaska)
- **Kusadasi** (Turkey)
- **Rhodes** and **Piraeus** (Greece)

Above: *A 1930s poster advertising* CUNARD*'s famous transatlantic liner the* Queen Mary.

THE STORY OF CRUISING

History

The notion of passengers sailing for pleasure, as opposed to mere travel necessity, became a reality in 1837 when Arthur Anderson and Brodie Wilcox founded the **Peninsular & Oriental Steam Navigation Company** – later abbreviated to **P&O**. About the same time an entrepreneur called **Samuel Cunard** also founded a transatlantic mail-carrier service that was to develop into the famous passenger line that still bears his name.

Cruising in the late 1800s and early 1900s meant mainly **transatlantic** crossings, with famous lines such as Cunard, White Star, Union-Castle, Hamburg-America, Norddeutscher Lloyd, Holland-America and French Line all racing for the prestigious Blue Riband award. But speed was not the only source of competition. The liners themselves became ever larger and more luxurious as aristocrats, movie stars and social climbers rubbed shoulders in opulent surroundings. Their presence provided valuable publicity in the battle for trade, but it was the hordes of **emigrants** in the cramped and lowly steerage sections who realistically financed the future of cruising.

Thankfully for those in cheaper quarters, such extremes of accommodation no longer exist and modern cruise ships allow all passengers equal access to public areas and amenities, irrespective of cabin grade. Even the *Queen Elizabeth 2*, which maintains a vestige of elitism with private bars for grill room diners, offers classless cruising compared to her formidable line of ancestors.

The primary purpose (and profit) of these maritime *grandes dames* was stolen by the rise of long-haul air travel through the 1960s and 70s, when the society-set became the jet-set and shipboard travel was considered *passé*. Cruising was able to initiate a revival by reinventing itself as a holiday experience and an escape from hassles and haste – although this was not so much by inflicting revenge on the airlines as entering into partnership with them, as fly/cruise packages have become an established part of cruising.

CRUISING WITH CUNARD

- CUNARD's first passenger (and mail) ship, *Britannia*, was a wooden paddle steamer whose maiden voyage from Liverpool to Boston in 1840 took two weeks. The novelist Charles Dickens later sailed on her and describes the crossing – in less than favourable terms – in *American Notes*.
- Nearly a century later, in the heyday of transatlantic travel, CUNARD's famous sisters, the *Queen Mary* and *Queen Elizabeth*, carried approximately 4000 passengers per week between Great Britain and the United States, saluting each other as they passed in the middle of the North Atlantic.

America this year
by
R.M.S. "Queen Mary"
Cunard
White Star

Left: *In 1938 the* Queen Mary *broke the record for a transatlantic crossing, taking just under four days to cross from New York to Land's End in Britain.*

I Name This Ship . . . (i)

The job of naming ships is often, although not always, bestowed upon ladies – and increasingly, celebrities. The following is a selection of contemporary cruise ships which have enjoyed a star-touched christening:

Crown Princess – **Sophia Loren**
Crystal Harmony – **Mary Tyler Moore**
Crystal Symphony – **Angela Lansbury**
Dreamward (now *Norwegian Dream*) – **Diana Ross**
France (now *Norway*) – **Mme Charles de Gaulle**
Nordic Prince (now *Carousel*) – **Ingrid Bergman**
Radisson Diamond – **Dame Kiri Te Kanawa**
Regal Princess – **Margaret Thatcher**
Royal Majesty – **Liza Minelli**
Royal Viking Sun – **James Stewart**
Seabourn Pride – **Shirley Temple Black**
Sovereign of the Seas – **Roslyn Carter**
Star Princess (now *Arcadia*) – **Audrey Hepburn**
Viking Serenade – **Whoopi Goldberg**
Windward (now *Norwegian Wind*) – **Barbara Bush**

The Future of Cruising

So where does the industry go from here? Certainly the mega-profits are with the mega-ships and many of the vessels intended for launch in the next few years will carry more than 2000 passengers and have a gross registered tonnage (grt) in excess of 70,000. There is even a proposal (by America's World City Corporation and Westin Hotels & Resorts) to construct four 250,000grt vessels, each with 21 decks, three accommodation towers and carrying 6200 passengers apiece. Although unlikely to appeal to traditionalists, the interesting thing about these

A LANDLUBBER'S LIST OF ESSENTIAL CRUISE SHIP TERMS

- To **embark** = To get on the ship
- To **disembark** = To get off the ship
- The **bow** = The front (pointed) end
- The **stern** = The back (blunt) end
- **For'ard** = Towards the front
- **Aft** = Towards the back
- **Port** = The left side (when facing the bow)
- **Starboard** = The right side (when facing the bow)
- A **tender** = A small boat used for ferrying passengers ashore when the ship is at anchor
- The **gangway** = The exterior stairway or access passage to and from the ship

huge 'floating resorts' is that they would offer not only extensive leisure amenities, but also tax-deductable **business** and **convention facilities**. There is every indication that corporate cruises may well become the business trips of the 21st century.

An important issue for the industry both now and in the future is the **environmental** impact of cruising, particularly given the frequency with which cruises now visit major conservation areas of the world. Critics stress high wastage levels, illegal dumping and sheer traffic volume in fragile areas as major causes for concern and it is a sad fact that cruising does reflect many aspects of today's 'disposable' world.

Another pressing issue for the industry is its gradual domination by a few powerful **conglomerates**, meaning that whichever line you eventually choose, you may be patronizing the same parent company. As an example, the giant Carnival Corporation currently owns not only Carnival Cruises, but several of its rivals, including Holland America, Windstar and Norwegian Cruise Line (NCL). It co-owns Seabourn and even has a substantial

Right: Carnival Destiny *– a member of the largest cruise fleet in the world and once the largest cruise ship in the world.*

Above: *The 105,000grt* Grand Princess *under construction. She is currently the world's largest passenger vessel.*

stake in the British cruise company, Airtours.

The industry is also now seeing increasing **standardization**, with ships of the same fleet offering identical products that reflect a corporate image – often carried through even to the names of the ships themselves. This trend can already be seen in the larger fleets of Carnival, Princess and Royal Caribbean and is likely to become even more prevalent as other companies modernize and upgrade their respective tonnage.

There is a move towards more casual, cheaper **family cruising** as lines seek to attract younger passengers, and especially young couples. **Dining options** look set to become more flexible and extensive, with 24-hour service and speciality restaurants appearing. Having exhausted some of the main sailing areas, companies are also looking to **expand** their itineraries. Unusual destinations will feature more prominently than ever before and the Far East and South Pacific look set to become major cruising regions.

In the light of this growing popularity, it is perhaps surprising that only about seven per cent of Americans – the industry's biggest market – have ever taken a cruise, yet surveys show that 85 per cent of those who do are keen to repeat the exercise. This bodes well for expansion and allows plenty of scope for future targeting.

But will the double-edged sword of tourism eventually strike cruising as it has other sectors, once the novelty has worn off and more original and distant experiences are sought? Can we perhaps expect a backlash away from the very big to the very small? Will the bottom fall out of the market and dozens of beached mega-ships lie as barren as the decaying hotels along the Spanish costas?

These are certainly considerations for the future.

I NAME THIS SHIP . . . (II)

A selection of contemporary cruise ships which have enjoyed a royal send off:
Cunard Princess (now *Rhapsody*) – **HRH Princess Grace of Monaco**
Hebridean Princess – **HRH the Duchess of York**
Majesty of the Seas – **HM Queen Sonja of Norway**
Nieuw Amsterdam – **HRH Princess Margriet**
Oriana – **HRH Queen Elizabeth II**
Queen Elizabeth 2 – **HRH Queen Elizabeth II**
Royal Princess – **HRH Princess Diana of Wales**
RMS St Helena – **HRH The Prince Andrew**
Sea Goddess II – **HRH Princess Caroline of Monaco**

2
Choosing a Cruise

Faced with the bewildering array of cruises available today on ships of every size and shape offering tantalizing opportunities to visit just about every part of the globe, choosing a cruise can seem like a daunting task. There are, however, some obvious categories by which cruises can be grouped, and a realization of these different groupings, along with the advantages and disadvantages each offers, can help make the task of choosing a cruise less confused. An understanding of such things as the different **types of ship** offering cruises, **where they go** and **what style of cruising** they offer can go a long way to helping you find the right holiday when you come to book your cruise.

First Considerations

Accepting that there is a cruise out there to suit just about every pocket and every requirement, there are certain fundamental considerations you should examine to begin your process of selection.

How Long?

With itineraries ranging from one-day trips to 150-day world circumnavigations, the length of a cruise obviously has an impact on budgeting considerations. Even if you have the financial resources to undertake a full world cruise, you have to consider whether you are prepared to shelve home, family or business commitments for that amount of time. For many people, several months is simply too long to be away, while a weekend may not be

Bargain Cruises

As cruising is such a fast-expanding area of tourism, substantial savings on brochure prices are always available. This particularly applies in the **USA**, where published brochure prices are invariably higher than the accepted 'going rate'. If you are able to plan well ahead, most cruise lines offer special rates for **early reservations**. At the other end of the scale, those able to wait until the **last minute** can pick up substantial bargains, providing they can be flexible in their demands. **Cruise brokers** (or consolidators) and companies specializing in last-minute discounts often advertise in the travel pages of national newspapers and on television information services.

Opposite: *The ultimate cruising experience – champagne and caviar aboard* CUNARD's Sea Goddess II.

long enough. For first-timers, a cruise of between **seven to ten days** duration should allow you time to settle in, find your way around the ship and have time to enjoy all the on-board facilities.

Time Planning

When calculating the number of days you have available for your cruise, take into account time spent **travelling** to join your vessel and any stopovers or nights in shoreside hotels. During a 14-day holiday, for example, only 10 of those days may actually be spent on the ship. On the other hand, check the amount of time allocated to **pre- and post-cruise arrangements**, as you won't see much of your disembarkation port if your transfer whisks you straight from the ship to the airport.

Budget

Cruise ships are, to a large extent, floating hotels, and in the same way that there is a huge difference between the cost of a week at the Seaview Guest House and the Ritz Hotel, so the price of a cruise – even for the same itinerary – may differ significantly from cruise line to cruise line and from vessel to vessel.

It is important, therefore, to establish how much you are prepared to spend on your holiday. If this is going to be a once-in-a-lifetime experience such as a honeymoon or anniversary, you might feel inclined to be more extravagant. On the other hand, if your cruise is simply a last-minute break or an extra treat to catch some winter sunshine, you will probably be looking for one of the cheaper deals available.

Location

Your choice of destination is all-important – and depends largely on your personality. Are you a sun-seeker or a culture-buff? A beach bum or a fitness freak? Do you want to be where the action is or get away from it all? You may find it worthwhile to do a little **background reading** on the places you are considering visiting. In addition to holiday brochures, seek out a few relevant travel books as these will give you a rather more unbiased insight into your choice of destination. (See also Chapter 6 for more about the world's most popular cruising regions.)

Commonly Asked Cruising Questions (2)

Q: *Where does the crew eat?*
A: Although you might spot officers and certain staff members eating at passenger buffets and even hosting tables in the passenger dining room, most members of the ship's company eat in designated crew dining areas. The food served is prepared by a team of crew chefs – although dishes served to the passengers are frequently duplicated.

Itinerary

Having decided on a region, take time to compare cruise itineraries, as ships sailing in the same part of the world may offer cruises of varying lengths and incorporating different ports of call. Be sure to take into account the amount of time you can expect to spend in each port and

the number of days you will be at sea. If the **destinations** are your priority, you will naturally want to include as many ports as possible, whereas if it is the **cruise experience** that appeals to you, you may be perfectly happy with four whole days out at sea. Be wary, however, of itineraries offering more than one destination per day. The idea of visiting 12 exotic islands during your seven-day cruise may be attractive, but you won't see much of them if you are only in each port for two or three hours.

Above: Royal Princess *arriving in Curacao.*

Out-of-Season Cruising

There is a lot to be said for travelling out of season: **prices** are often substantially lower; **flights** aren't over-booked; **destinations** are less busy – and with fewer tourists you're more likely to get the 'real feel' of the place; and as the ship is generally less crowded **service** should be more attentive. In addition, there are often some very nice financial incentives for last-minute reservations. The **downside** of travelling off-peak is the fact that certain shoreside **attractions** may be closed, shore **excursions** may be cancelled and the **weather** may be far from ideal.

What Time of Year?

As with all holidays, cruise dates are priced according to demand and expected weather conditions, with high season, mid-season and low season prices. The best deals are to be found when demand has dropped but the weather is still potentially good. Those with flexible schedules might wish to take advantage of Alaska 'bargains' in early May or a Caribbean cruise in November. Parents with school-children would do well to book for periods such as late August or early September, which tends to be mid-season rather than high season.

CRUISING AT CHRISTMAS

The idea of a pampered Christmas/New Year cruise may be appealing, but be warned that **prices** are generally considerably **higher** during the festive season and this is unlikely to be reflected in what you actually get for your money. The ship may be beautifully **decorated**, but the **food** is unlikely to be much of a variation on the regular menu (*whatever* the chef says!) and it is not a coincidence that more **complaints** are aired during Christmas cruises than at any other time of the year – perhaps due to the number of passengers who came on a cruise to avoid celebrating Christmas in the first place.

Styles of Cruises

Do you normally work in a business suit – and therefore relish the prospect of wearing something more relaxed on holiday? Do you live in jeans – and therefore enjoy the occasional chance to dress up? Are you looking forward to a romantic break? Or are you looking for an action-packed adventure?

The different styles of cruising available on different cruise lines vary enormously, and finding a style to suit your expectations is a vital part of choosing a cruise. Young first-time cruisers and families, for example, are often attracted to the bigger ships with their flash public rooms and extensive facilities; more mature or experienced cruisers might prefer the discreet service and yacht-like ambience of a very small vessel; and, subject to variations in interests and budgets, the majority will probably opt for something in between. It is, however, important to relate your expectations of a cruise to the cost of the holiday and the way the cruise is represented. All too often, potential cruisers compare ships while forgetting to compare fares.

Dressing Up or Dressing Down?

Cruising is one of the last bastions for dressing up: the Captain's Welcome, the formal cocktail parties and the Gala Dinner all form part of the image of traditional cruising. As a rule of thumb, the **Baltic**, the **Black Sea** and other cruising areas with a comfortably mild seasonal climate tend to attract more elegantly dressed passengers than the Caribbean or peak-season Mediterranean. **World cruises** on prestigious vessels also lean to a level of formality that reflects the cost of the trip.

To really indulge yourself, go for SEABOURN, CRYSTAL, CUNARD, RADISSON SEVEN SEAS or SILVERSEA cruise lines – all companies found at the higher end of the

market. However, formal evenings are also scheduled on most mainstream vessels, and while this may mean little more than a clean t-shirt to some guests, others enjoy making an effort. If you enjoy dressing up, then avoid low-budget family cruises and expeditions and trips where unusual destinations are the focus.

If you prefer the emphasis to be on **informality**, it is worth remembering that on most vessels beachwear (weather permitting) is commonplace through the day – it is the evenings that betray how formal or informal the dress code is on a ship. Opt for destination-oriented holidays, low-budget deals, family cruises, 'party' trips and alternative styles of cruising (such as by cargo ship or sailing ship). For a more up-scale yet 'elegantly casual' experience, consider the fleet of RENAISSANCE CRUISES or the modern sail-cruisers of WINDSTAR. In general, a browse through the **brochures** should give you a good indication of a vessel's lifestyle.

Party or Relaxation Mode?

If you are looking for **action**, go for the big ships with a younger or mixed age group found on lines such as CARNIVAL, PRINCESS, NORWEGIAN, CELEBRITY or ROYAL CARIBBEAN. Very small vessels may have little or no nightlife, and passengers on destination-oriented cruises

Above: *A musical evening on the formal, five-star luxury* Europa, *flagship of the* HAPAG-LLOYD *fleet.*
Opposite: *A bright breakfast on* Radisson Diamond *– a ship at the luxury end of the market.*

THE CAPTAIN'S COCKTAIL PARTY

Shaking hands with hundreds of people in a single evening has always been part of the captain's job. Some ships, however, are so large that they have to cheat a little, with the captain greeting half the guests in one lounge and the second-in-command greeting the rest in another. PRINCESS CRUISES has even taken to holding the party in the atrium lobby of its newest vessels with no official greeting and hand-shaking at all.

Right: *Winner by a nose – a sun-burnt nose. Fun and games aboard* Viking Serenade.
Opposite: *Well-equipped and professionally supervized gymnasiums are found on most new and larger ships.*

tend to be early birds rather than night owls. The nationality of your fellow passengers and crew can also make a huge difference. Ships staffed by Italian or Greek officers and marketed mainly to South American or central European travellers often enjoy a particularly good party atmosphere.

If you'd prefer to **unwind** rather than rave it up, opt for mid-sized to large ships catering particularly to the over-50 age group (good examples are CRYSTAL, SEABOURN, CUNARD and HOLLAND AMERICA). If it's just a quiet spot to curl up with a good book you are seeking, most vessels will be able to provide that, but if you also want anonymity, avoid very small ships where your privacy is bound to be threatened. Don't forget to take the itinerary into account – lots of days at sea are more conducive to relaxation than a hectic sightseeing schedule.

On-board Facilities

When choosing a cruise, **sports** enthusiasts may well look for a gymnasium and/or jogging track, together with options such as aerobics classes and watersports; a decent **laundry** might be a requisite for some guests, while others would not wish to sail without a well-equipped ship's **hospital**. The kids will probably be happy as long as the **swimming pool** is filled.

EXTRAS HIDDEN

Be sure to **double-check** that facilities indicated on a ship's plan are, in fact, in regular operation. It is not unknown for vessels to use their watersports platform solely for their launches when in port or for the card room to have been transformed into somebody's office. If a particular facility is important to you – and especially to the point of being a deciding factor between one ship and another – it is worth a phone call to the cruise line to check that it really does exist and is functioning properly.

Fellow Passengers

Your fellow passengers could be more important to the enjoyment of your cruise than you realize, for ideally you will want to select a cruise where you will feel at home among like-minded individuals. Unsurprisingly, the more expensive ships attract a higher proportion of older passengers and high-earning professionals; academics are inclined to opt for unusual itineraries and expeditions; and young couples and families generally head for the sun-and-fun cheapies.

But there are other less obvious factors to take into account. For example, on ships where yours is not the primary **language** or which cater to passengers of various nationalities, you could find yourself with communication difficulties and even a feeling of alienation. It will be harder to participate in activities or get to know your fellow guests, and your guided tours may be conducted in a foreign language – or even worse, tediously translated into several languages. **Cultural differences** may also come to the fore – those who prefer not to be cajoled into deck games by bouncy, permanently smiling cheerleader-types would do well to avoid most of the mega-ships sailing out of Florida; US passengers, on the other hand, are likely to find European ships to be tobacco-fogged and possibly too eclectic for their tastes.

WHO GOES WHERE

- **British** passengers tend to feel at home on the ships of AIRTOURS, CUNARD, FRED OLSEN, P&O and the recently formed cruising divisions of SAGA and THOMSON HOLIDAYS; P&O, with its frequent passages 'down under' and vessels based in Antipodean waters, also features prominently in the **Australian** and **New Zealand** cruise market.
- **German**-speakers predominate on the cruises of, among others, HAPAG-LLOYD, DEUTSCHE SEEREEDEREI, DEILMANN REEDEREI and PHOENIX REISEN.
- **Italian** and **Spanish** passengers head for the ships of MSC, COSTA and multi-lingual Greek-based companies such as ROYAL OLYMPIC; and the *Mermoz* and *Le Ponant* attract a mainly **French**-speaking clientele.
- The established **Japanese** market is headed by lines such as NYK and MITSUI OSK, with STAR CRUISE also a forerunner in the growing Asian marketplace.

Crowded Out

If you are gregarious, you might appreciate the fact that **larger ships** carry more people, with the greater choice of new acquaintances this affords. But bear in mind that it also means a more impersonal – and potentially, lonely – cruise. The sheer number of passengers on a big ship can result in long lines for self-service buffets, crowded pool areas and delays getting off the vessel (especially in tender ports and on disembarkation day). **Smaller ships** have a more intimate atmosphere: you will encounter the same passengers regularly and are more likely to make new friends. However, this may not appeal to those seeking a more anonymous cruise experience.

Types of Ship

While there are numerous variations in passenger ships operating around the globe, all vessels can be categorized in terms of **size, age** and the **price** of their cruises, three factors which go a long way to helping you understand what to expect from a cruise.

Size

The main advantages of **bigger ships** are that they can do things on a broader and grander scale. They invariably offer more diverse **facilities** and **activities** for all age groups and generally offer a higher calibre of **entertainment**, including glamorous productions and celebrity acts. Very small ships have neither the space nor the budget to accommodate shows of this type. In addition, bigger ships (especially older ones) tend to be more **stable** and can weather a storm better.

Bigger ships also tend to be **cheaper.** Rather like the difference between a supermarket and a corner shop, the 'big boys' are more able to peddle special offers by dealing in bulk. The downside, of course, is that you are unlikely to get the same one-to-one **service** as on a smaller vessel and the whole product is geared to the middle-market, with much less consideration of individual requirements.

Smaller ships, on the other hand, score on **intimacy** and **flexibility**. They are more likely to be able to **dock alongside** in port, thus reducing the need to use launches. This is a definite boon for less-mobile passengers, and makes access to and from the vessel much easier and quicker. By the same

token, smaller ships can get to places such as **remote islands**, **narrow inlets** and **inland waterways** that are out of reach to larger ships.

Another advantage of smaller ships is that they are more **accessible**. Whether fetching your sunglasses from your cabin or adjourning from the restaurant to the bar, you will appreciate the fact that this doesn't involve a 20-minute excursion. On the other hand, smaller ships – especially very small, yacht-like vessels – can become rather **claustrophobic** to those who like a lot of space. Note, however, that the standard cabins of petite deluxe vessels are generally far more spacious than those on bigger ships.

Age

Compare a ship to a car or a house and you will appreciate that vessels of different ages also offer a very different feel even though they may be of comparable size. For the purposes of this guide, 1970 is taken as an approximate division between old and new.

Among the benefits of **newer ships** is the **space** they have to offer. They tend to have a brighter, more airy, feel, with larger and more accessible public rooms, corridors and stairwells. They can offer the latest in **modern**

Chill Factor

The advantages of modern technology can occasionally run away with themselves – on certain ships you can sometimes find the ship's air-conditioning blasting so cold that a light jacket may be required to sit in the showroom, even if it's a roasting 30°C (86°F) outside.

Left: *RCI's 73,000grt* Monarch of the Seas *(top) and 48,000grt* Nordic Empress. **Opposite**: *On board the massive 100,000grt* Carnival Destiny.

Relating Size to Age

When you consider the wildly prohibitive construction cost of a new ship today (the *Carnival Destiny* cost approximately $400 million), it is understandable that only a cluster of companies can actually afford to build new vessels. Because these tend to be the very lines that also dominate the 'mega-market' it follows that most of the very large ships are at the newer end of the scale – with the notable exception of the *Queen Elizabeth 2* (1969) and the *Norway* (1962). As a general rule, the major cruise lines (usually US-based) operate most of the new tonnage, whereas the ships of smaller (and especially European) companies are often well into middle-age.

ASKING A LADY'S AGE

Indications of the age of your intended vessel will be found in the cruise line **brochure**. It may even state the year the ship entered service, but if not, a quick call to the cruise line in question should provide the answer. Be aware, however, that ships are often **re-named** when they are sold from one company to another, so although a vessel may have been in operation only two years under its current title, it could have had five previous names and been launched in 1928! Serious researchers should consult the *Lloyd's Registry of Shipping*, found in public reference libraries.

technology, which might include automatic sliding doors, video arcades, state-of-the-art elevators and interactive cabin gadgetry. On the other hand, while newer ships often have larger public rooms, **standard cabins** have become smaller. This reflects the changing face of cruising: years ago, cruises tended to be longer and offered less entertainment, whereas nowadays cruises have become shorter but offer more entertainment, putting more emphasis on lavish public areas and less on private space. Anyone wanting spacious accommodation on modern ships should consider paying more for a high grade suite. As a rule, newer ships offer generally fewer cabin **categories** – an advantage when the many variations on older vessels often leads to confusion.

Older ships, however, still have much to offer. One of the most noticeable drawbacks of newer ships is the disappearance of **deck space** around the sides and at the stern. This can be a real blow to anyone who enjoys the traditional circumferential stroll, and there are few sights more spectacular than watching a port recede from an aft deck. The compensation on newer ships is that they offer more **private balconies**.

Older ships are also generally more **substantial**, built with a deeper draft which allows them to take the weather well, while most modern ships have a shallow draft and some are decidedly top-heavy, making them susceptible to rolling. The standards of **craftsmanship** are also commonly much higher on older vessels, which gives them an intangible but appealing character, and the fact that older ships are mostly powered by steam turbine engines mean that they tend to be **quieter** than their modern diesel counterparts. New diesel engines, however, are more fuel efficient and vibration levels are increasingly being reduced with each technological development.

COMMONLY ASKED CRUISING QUESTIONS (3)

Q: *Does the crew ever get off the ship?*
A: Although they don't necessarily get off every time in every port, crew members do get time to explore. It's worth remembering that on regular itineraries your ship may be in the same port every few days, so the crew will know the place well and can always point you in the right direction for bars, eateries and telephones.

Price Differences

Considering the vast differences in cost between cruises, you might question whether one company is wildly overcharging or the other giving wonderful value for

Left: *AIRTOUR's budget family cruiser* Carousel, *launched in 1971, alongside at Mahon in Minorca.*

what may appear to be basically the same cruise. But the overall experience is made up of so many factors that ships with the same itinerary could never offer exactly the same cruise any more than a camp site, holiday cottage and five-star hotel could provide exactly the same weekend break.

In general, the **less** you pay for your cruise, the more you will be enticed to part with cash on the ship to pay for **extras**. Shore excursions, gratuities and drinks are standard extras on most vessels, but those offering really cheap deals are much more likely to put pressure on the sale of tours, bingo cards and souvenirs, as well as pushing their gambling facilities. At the upper end of the range, on the other hand, packages may be inclusive of gratuities, shore excursions, food and even drink. Another common factor on cheaper cruises is that they are more likely to be **noisier**, with more announcements, activities, louder music and children.

Ironically, the more you pay, the less **entertainment** you may get. Small deluxe vessels rarely provide nightly shows or organized activities. If you are looking for entertainment *and* upscale cruising, go for the top suites on ships such as the *Crystal Harmony*, *Crystal Symphony*, *Europa*, *Royal Viking Sun* and *Queen Elizabeth 2*.

CHAIN CRUISING

An increasingly apparent modern theme is that ships tend to be more **standardized** and lacking in individual characteristics – even offering identical layouts to other ships in their fleet. Rather like buying a burger from an international fast food chain, you know exactly what to expect, wherever you may find yourself in the world. Of course, the downside of such predictability is that you may also end up eating from an identical menu and watching identical entertainment (same show, different cast) whether you are on Mega-ship 'A' in the Bahamas or Mega-ship 'B' in the Baltic. Older ships, even those of the same fleet, offer a cruise experience with features unique to that vessel. For better or worst, at least it will be different.

Right: Royal Viking Sun *– one of the most luxurious and highly rated ships in the cruising market.*

> **COMMONLY ASKED CRUISING QUESTIONS (4)**
>
> **Q:** *What is the procedure if I need to complain?*
> **A:** Take your complaint up as soon as possible with the person responsible for that particular area of service. For example, complaints relating to the cleaning of your cabin should be directed to the Housekeeper; restaurant problems should be brought to the attention of the maître d'; and issues relating to ship-board procedures and accounts should be raised at the Purser's desk. If you do not receive satisfaction, insist on meeting with the hotel manager. Technical (air-conditioning, plumbing, electrical) problems should be reported at the main information (usually the Purser's) desk. You may also wish to mention your complaint on your end-of-cruise questionnaire.

The more **expensive** the cruise, the more **personal service** you should receive. On deluxe yacht-like vessels the passenger-crew ratio is almost one to one, while on very big ships (such as the *Crystal Harmony*, *Crystal Symphony*, *Queen Elizabeth 2* or *Royal Viking Sun*) the most expensive suites include the services of a private butler. Similarly, the more you pay for your accommodation, the more **space** you should enjoy, with the best suites comprising such things as a lounge, private balcony, extra bathroom and whirlpool bath.

The price of your cruise may affect the standard of **food and dining** amenities you receive. The *Queen Elizabeth 2*, for example, has five restaurants served by three different galleys, each offering accommodation-related levels of service and cuisine. It's worth noting, however, that top-grade cabins on many mainstream ships do not offer any dining advantages at all.

BOOKING YOUR CRUISE

While it is possible to book your holiday directly with a cruise line, there is rarely a financial advantage to this and most passengers prefer the convenience of discussing options with their local **travel agent**.

For specific advice, you may wish to seek out an agency that specializes in cruise ship travel. Such agents

– increasingly termed 'Cruise Consultants' – include members of **CLIA** (Cruise Line International Association) or **NACOA** (North American Cruise-Only Agencies) in the United States and **PSARA** (Passenger Shipping Association of Retail Agents) or the Guild of Professional Cruise Agents in the United Kingdom.

Decoding Cruise Brochures

You can take the first step to determining which ships might best suit you simply by browsing through a few brochures. Cruise line brochures tell you more than you may realize about the line in question – far more than is divulged by the text alone.

Firstly, consider **the brochure itself**. Does it feel and look expensive? Then, most probably, so is the line. Then there is the **content**. Destinations sell cruises, but the true indications of the style of the cruise are to be deduced not from pictures of exotic lands, but from those of the ship itself – and, most especially, the **people**. Budget publicity tends to emphasise the value rather than the exclusivity of the cruise. If you see prices splashed liberally throughout, almost certainly it's a budget deal. Other good indications are how casually or formally the passengers are **dressed**, the **ages** of the passengers depicted, and whether **children** are featured. Above all, look at the **faces**, and ask yourself if these are your sort of people.

Another useful aspects of a brochure is the **deck plan**, by which you should be able to make out cabin shapes and the location of facilities. Finally, before parting with your deposit, take time to read the **small print** at the back of the brochure. This will contain vital information, including points unique to cruising, such as the company's right to omit or change ports and your ineligibility for a refund if you jump ship or miss the boat.

Package Deals Versus Independent Travel

Fly/cruise packages are becoming the norm for cruising holidaymakers, but if you don't require every element of a package (you may live near the port or can stay with

Important Booking Tips

- Bear in mind that some travel agents may have a financial interest in promoting certain vessels or may even be affiliated to a specific cruise line. For a more **unbiased** picture, seek the advice of several different agents.
- Shop around for **bargains**. Some cruise lines offer deals to repeat cruisers, singles prepared to cruise 'stand-by', seniors and families.
- Be sceptical of **unsolicited letters** congratulating you on winning a 'free' cruise. The catch is often that the two- or three-night cruise is free, but that flights, transfers and everything else are not!
- Take out full **cancellation insurance**. Most cruise lines will charge a hefty fee (up to 100%) for cruises cancelled within 30 days of the departure date.
- Check whether **flights**, **transfers** and **port charges** are included in the price of your cruise.
- Don't forget to state any special accommodation or dietary requirements at the time of booking.

Cruising when Pregnant

Cruise ships may refuse passage to women in the **third trimester** of pregnancy. Pregnant women are therefore strongly advised to check the policy of their prospective cruise line before making a reservation.

friends rather than a designated hotel), then you might prefer to take a 'cruise only' deal and handle your own travel arrangements. Essentially, fly/cruise packages are a good option for bargain hunters and those who prefer the security of organized group transportation.

One of the advantages of package deals is that cruise lines strike **special deals** with airlines and may sometimes charter an entire plane (some cruise companies even operate their own aircraft). Fly/cruise packages also commonly include **transfers** to and from the airport, hotel and ship and your **baggage** should emerge at your cabin without you having to oversee its arrival personally. Also, in the unlikely event of your cruise being **cancelled** or disrupted, those on a fly/cruise package are usually entitled to reimbursement and accommodation in hotels at no extra charge.

On the other hand, there are a number of drawbacks to fly/cruise packages. Low-budget flights often entail changes to different aircraft in remote airports or an inconvenient departure time. Neither are you likely to be able to reserve aircraft seats or upgrade (unless such an option is part of the deal). In addition, some people may also find it frustrating having to wait for groups of fellow passengers to assemble for every transfer or being taken on a sightseeing trip (whether you want to or not!) to fill in the time between your flight and joining/leaving your ship.

Below: *A typically compact standard cabin.*

Choosing a Cabin

Rooms aboard ships are known as cabins, suites or staterooms and vary enormously depending on the grade and the ship in question. **Suites or staterooms** suggest superior accommodation, but be aware that the term 'suite' is often indiscriminately used, irrespective of size, location

Above: *A mini-suite, with a private balcony, on a larger cruise ship.*

and facilities offered. Genuine suites are spacious, luxurious and expensive compared to regular cabins – they may include balconies, large double beds, walk-in closets and occasionally, a whirlpool bath. Amenities might include such things as a television and video, music system, refrigerator, safe and the services of a personal butler. Suites tend to be found on the higher decks of a vessel, a great place for wonderful views but less comfortable in rough seas.

Among more moderately priced **cabins**, *en suite* bathroom facilities are a fairly standard feature, but bear in mind that it may house little more than a toilet, sink and shower-head. In general, ship cabins are small, although they will usually house a vanity unit, bedside table, drawers, perhaps an armchair or sofa, a telephone (for in-ship and satellite calls), a radio and, increasingly, a television.

Those designated as **outer** (sometimes called 'outside' or 'exterior') cabins will have a view, although it may be restricted by a lifeboat or walkway (check the brochure). On lower decks, these cabins may have traditional round portholes, while those on upper decks usually boast large square-shaped 'picture' windows.

Inner ('inside' or 'interior') cabins will be the least expensive. These have no windows and, hence, no view, and can feel claustrophobic, but for sea-sickness sufferers they do offer the most stable accommodation.

Cabins at either end of the ship also tend to be cheaper than those in the middle as the extremities are less stable in strong seas and are subject to greater noise. Lower deck cabins towards the stern may suffer bad vibration and engine noise, while occupants of those at the bow may be awakened at some unearthly hour by the dropping anchor.

A Better Outlook

Newer ships tend to have **picture windows** in cabins instead of portholes. These afford a better view and more sunlight, but are permanently sealed. The advantage of an older **porthole** is that it can often be opened to let in the bracing sea air. The disadvantage is that, if you forget to close it, in rough weather it can also let in the sea water! For **nervous** sailors, a porthole situated close to the water level may be worse than no window at all, as the view in rough seas is second only to watching a front-loader washing machine going through its cycle.

3
Life Aboard

Day-to-day life aboard a cruise ship can seem strange at first, especially for those more familiar with land-based holidays. There is little, however, that is too daunting – first-time passengers often find the unusual way of life quite exciting, while old hands look forward to the traditions and rituals with affection. While good living and relaxation are often the key to a great cruising holiday, the most common complaint of passengers at the end of their trip is that they didn't have time to fit everything in.

Crossing the Equator

No equator crossing at sea is complete without an appearance by King Neptune (alias the Cruise Director) and his entourage of mermaids and other sea creatures (alias the social and entertainment staff). In keeping with ancient sacrificial rites, at least one member of the ship's company will end up in the swimming pool – possibly after a poolside operation by a 'mad surgeon'. Passengers are often included in the ceremony – which usually involves being 'blessed' by King Neptune.

Preparations

Passports and Visas

For all cruises beyond the coastal waters of your own nation, you will need a full **passport**, valid for the duration of your intended voyage. You may find you have to renew your passport if it is due to expire within six months of your trip. If this happens, remember to apply for or renew the necessary visas. Your travel agent and/or cruise line should be able to advise you of **visa** requirements for your intended itinerary and, for a service fee, may help you obtain them. The responsibility – and cost – of securing visas is, however, always that of the passenger.

Health Precautions and Insurance

Subject to your intended itinerary, you may need to obtain valid **proof of immunization** against specific diseases. Failure to provide this could result in you being

Opposite: *Style and glamour on the sweeping tiered decks of* Crystal Symphony.

ORGANIZING IMMUNIZATIONS

It is important to leave yourself enough time to obtain the necessary inoculations before the commencement of your cruise – for example, the preliminary dose of **hepatitis B** or **typhoid** vaccine should be given eight weeks prior to sailing and a **yellow fever** shot should be administered three weeks beforehand.

denied permission to disembark, particularly in high risk areas such as Africa. Details of immunization requirements for your proposed countries of call may be obtained from your **doctor** or a **medical centre**. Bear in mind that requirements are subject to change and that obtaining proof of immunizations, like visas, is the responsibility of the passenger.

Adequate travel, and especially health, **insurance** is also a necessary consideration when planning your cruise. Shipboard medical centres charge for their services and the cost of landing emergency cases for treatment at shoreside hospitals – particularly if helicopter transportation is involved – can be astronomical. There is usually an insurance option offered when you make your reservation. If you do not wish to take it, make sure that you are independently covered for any eventuality. This applies particularly if you intend to travel on a vessel (such as a cargo ship) that does not have medical staff and facilities.

What to Pack

Travel as light as you can – cabins rarely have huge amounts of storage space and you won't want to deal with too much luggage if you have to make connecting flights and hotel stopovers. The following guidelines should make life easier and your luggage lighter:

- **Pack only comfortable clothes**. Even formal attire can be comfortable and you should be able to enjoy wearing it the entire evening.
- **Never pack bulky garments**. Even if you are cruising the Antarctic or Alaska, multiple layers of thin garments are more effective than a thick sweater or overcoat. Take a light jacket or cardigan for the evening chill or force nine air-conditioning.
- **Respect local dress codes**. Pack clothing you can comfortably wear aboard and ashore without causing offence. On the ship, a light cover-up over swimwear is a good idea for eating by the pool or strolling through public areas. When ashore, bear in mind the culture of the place you are visiting. A cool, long-sleeved shirt and

ELECTRICITY ON SHIPS

Most ships marketed in the **USA** will have 110V outlets in their cabins, while **European-based** vessels may employ 220V. Your ship's voltage is normally stated at the back of the cruise brochure. If necessary, pack an appropriate **travel plug** and/or converter.

Left: *Informality and relaxation are key elements of a comfortable cruise.*

lightweight long trousers or a flowing skirt are universally acceptable.

• **Mix 'n' match**. Avoid outfits that cannot be worn on more than one occasion. Unless the ship is very formal, a business suit or blazer with co-ordinating trousers can be worn by men on most evenings. A matching skirt/slacks/top combination for women is far more versatile than an individual dress. Jogging suits, Bermuda-style shorts, a classic sports- or t-shirt and sunhat are acceptable forms of daywear on any ship.

• **Cut back on shoes**. Shoes, and particularly, ladies' high heels, are a menace to pack – so be ruthless. Take no more than three pairs (and that includes the shoes you wear up the gangway). One of these should be a pair of flat, comfortable, rubber-soled deck shoes or trainers. Unless you are on a very casual ship, you will also require a pair of evening shoes. Select a classic style and neutral colour that compliments your entire evening wardrobe. For sun 'n' fun-style cruises, sandals are the obvious third choice, while a strong pair of water-resistant walking shoes might be a worthy substitute in colder climes.

• **Choose materials carefully**. Natural fibres 'breathe' better than synthetics and are a cool choice for sightseeing

DON'T FORGET . . .

• Your **important documents** – passport, visas and proof of vaccinations (if applicable), ship/airline tickets and any transfer tickets.
• Your **driving licence** – required if you intend renting a car.
• A sufficient quantity of prescribed **medications**.
• A spare pair of **glasses** or **contact lenses**.
• **PADI card** or other recognized proof of certification if you intend to scuba dive.
• Video camera **batteries** and recharger.
• Small **travel alarm clock**.
• **Sunglasses**.
• **Binoculars** (if you intend bird or wildlife spotting).
• **Camera**.

Laundry Services

Most ships offer some kind of laundry service, including **dry-cleaning**, although you will normally have to pay for them. Certain items will cost more than others and same day service costs are usually extra – there should be a price list in your cabin. You can **save money** by hand washing in your bathroom, storing dirty clothes until you get home or using the free self-service **launderette**.

in tropical climes, but they are prone to wrinkling. Cotton/polyester blends, synthetic silks, wool knits, rayon crêpe, chiffon and sequinned fabrics don't wrinkle, and are therefore a practical choice for evening wear.

- **Wash 'n' wear**. Keep underclothes and casual garments to a minimum. You may well buy new swimwear, t-shirts or 'logo' casual clothes during your cruise, and most ships have laundry facilities. An easy way to reduce your turnover of basics is simply rinsing small items and hanging them in the bathroom overnight.
- **Leave the crown jewels at home**. Although cruising is basically crime-free, daytime wear on even the most prestigious vessels is casual and it is extremely unwise to sport expensive jewellery or possessions when exploring ports of call. As an alternative, wear costume jewellery.
- **Keep electrical appliances to a minimum**. Hairdryers and travel irons are bulky to pack and such items are often available on board. If you do take electrical appliances, you may also need a travel plug and/or converter.
- **Don't carry too many books**. Most ships have a lending library and a small selection of books may be sold in the on-board gift shop. Limit yourself to one or two paperbacks which you can donate to the ship's library when you leave.

Below: *The library aboard the* Queen Elizabeth 2 *– the largest floating library in the world.*

• **Downsize your toiletry items**. Many toiletry items can be extremely bulky. Don't forget that many ships provide basic toiletries free of charge and sell additional items in their on-board shops.

• **Keep important things in hand**. When travelling to or from the ship, never pack money, travellers cheques, valuables, travel documents (such as passports and tickets) or vital medications in your check-in baggage. Such items should always be carried in your hand luggage.

Last-Minute Details

When your **cruise tickets** arrive, double-check all details, including dates and times. If you spot a mistake, contact your travel agent or operator straight away so that it can be rectified as soon as possible. Complete and return any **forms** as requested and fill in as much as possible of any other forms to be taken with you. This will save time when you finally reach the check-in desk.

Write your name, ship and cabin number (if known) clearly on **luggage tags** and attach one to every item of baggage. It is also worth including the name and contact information of the **shipping agency** used by your vessel in its embarkation port, as waylaid luggage may be forwarded via the agents. In case the outer tag becomes detached, remember also to include contact information on the inside of each case. You may also want to leave the ship's satellite **phone** or **fax number** with a friend or relative back home, so you can be contacted in the event of an emergency.

Joining your ship

Getting There

Most passengers book their holiday as part of a **fly/cruise package**, inclusive of flights, transfers and, possibly, hotel accommodation. If this applies to you, look out for a 'meet-and-greet' member of ground staff at your destination airport. They should be holding a sign with the name of your ship or cruise line written on it. Make yourself known to this person and after you have claimed your baggage, after which you will be escorted with the

Passport Control

When checking into your ship, you will probably be expected to **hand over** your passport for safe-keeping in the Purser's office. First-time cruisers may be reluctant to do this, but this is an accepted shipboard practice and it means the passports of all passengers and crew can then be made available for inspection whenever required – such as six o'clock in the morning when the immigration officials come aboard! Should you require your passport (e.g. to cash travellers' cheques), you can claim it from the Purser's desk prior to going ashore.

Money On Board

• You will be required to register a **credit card** with the Pursers' office in order to open your **shipboard account**. This allows you to sign for drinks, shore excursions and other non-inclusive items during your cruise. An alternative form of deposit may be acceptable, but check this before booking.

• Although a minority of vessels may revert to cash sales on the last evening as bills are finalized, **cashless** cruising has been adopted by almost all lines. At the end of your cruise, an **itemized** copy of your account will be delivered to your cabin and, presuming there is no cause for query, the total will automatically be charged to your registered credit card.

other passengers to some waiting buses to be taken to your ship (or hotel, if a pre-cruise stay is included).

If you are making your **own way** to the ship, you may need to show your travel documents at the port gates to gain admittance. Taxis are usually permitted to take you as close to your vessel as possible, although this may be no further than a terminal building. In ports such as Miami, a small fee will secure the services of a **porter** to help you with your luggage. Porter assistance or luggage carts will not necessarily be available in every port.

THE WAITING GAME

When you get to your cabin you may have to wait for your luggage to arrive. Here are a few useful things you can do while you are waiting:

- Study the ship's **Daily Programme** which will probably be in your cabin.
- Check to see if **refreshments** are being served, and get there before they stop!
- Try your **cabin keys** (or card) in the lock. If your key doesn't appear to work, ask a steward for assistance.
- If your cabin does not have a **safe**, arrange a personal deposit box with the Purser.
- If the **library** is open, take out a couple of books or videos before the most popular choices disappear.
- **Explore** the ship.

Checking-In

As with a hotel, you need to check in to your ship before you board. This usually takes place in the **terminal building** or a **departure hall** close to the ship. If you arrive outside the designated time or you are a passenger on a very small vessel, you may be required to check-in at the **Pursers'** or **reception desk** on the ship. Where the majority of passengers are participating in a pre-cruise package, check-in formalities may even be conducted at your **hotel**.

If you are on a fly/cruise package, your **ship's representatives** or **ground staff** will escort you through the whole procedure. If you are making your own way to the ship, remember to allow yourself enough time to get there, check in and embark (the gangway is usually raised half an hour before the actual sailing time).

Settling In

The **first evening** of your cruise is likely to be spent unpacking and familiarizing yourself with your cabin and the ship. Cruise lines know that many passengers are tired from travelling and so the first night tends to be deliberately low key. The dress code will be **casual** on even the dressiest vessel, a **taster show** giving a sample of forthcoming attractions and productions is often presented in the main lounge, and the Cruise Director may give a **brief orientation** of the vessel and introduce the members of the **cruise staff** and concessionaires, such as the shop, casino and spa managers.

Left: *The* MV Vesteralen, *well equipped with accessible lifeboats in the event of an emergency.*

The Passenger Safety Drill

The passenger safety drill is a mandatory requirement on all ships and, in accordance with international maritime law, must take place within the first 24 hours of your cruise. The time of the drill should be listed in your copy of the daily programme and announcements will be made shortly before the emergency signal (seven short blasts and one long blast of the ship's whistle and alarm bells) is sounded, advising all passengers to collect their **life jackets** from their cabins and proceed to their allocated **muster station**. Your life jacket will probably be stowed in your wardrobe or closet and your muster station letter or number will be indicated on the front of your life-jacket and/or on a **safety notice** on the back of your cabin or bathroom door.

This safety drill usually lasts no longer than 30 minutes and should be taken seriously. Smoking, drinking and the use of elevators are not allowed during the drill (in a real emergency elevators may be immobilized). Passengers who have physical difficulties getting to their station should advise a crew member, such as their steward, who will arrange assistance.

The Daily Programme

Every evening, a programme listing times, places and useful information concerning the next day's agenda will probably be slipped under your cabin door. Many ships also display the same information on one of the **in-house television** channels. Among the most important things listed on this are:

- The **opening hours** of on-board facilities such as the surgery, library, fitness centre and beauty salon.
- **Departure and return times** of the organized shore excursions.
- **Restaurant and buffet times** and the evening **dress code**.
- Times and locations of all the organized on-board **activities.**
- Details of the evening's **entertainment**.
- **Background information** about the next port.
- Currency **exchange rates**.

Commonly Asked Cruising Questions (5)

Q: *Will I be able to visit the bridge, galley or engine room?*

A: Some ships (mainly passenger-cargo or very small vessels) operate an 'open bridge' policy, allowing passengers to visit at any time, but this is never the case on large mainstream cruise ships, where access is strictly by invitation only. Sometime during your cruise, however, an escorted visit to the bridge may be scheduled (keep your eye on the daily programme). A tour of the ship's galley (including the cooking, preparation and storage areas) may also be arranged, as well as an escorted visit to the Engine Control Room. For insurance reasons, however, the engines themselves are almost always out of bounds to passengers.

Who's Who On The Ship

Most cruise ships divide their personnel into three **divisions** (officers, staff and crew) and four **departments** (deck, engine, hotel and medical). **Officers** constitute the governing body of the ship – higher ranking officers invariably sport more stripes on their sleeve or epaulet than their junior counterparts, and they also boast a lower numbered title – a first engineer, for example, ranks higher than a second engineer. Certain positions may warrant **petty officer** status – a mid-way rank between officer and crew member.

The second category is that of **staff** – a term used to describe a large portion of a ship's hotel department. Entertainers, social staff members, shop and casino employees, photographers, sports instructors, beauty salon and spa personnel are all staff members. The third division constitutes the **crew** – the largest division on any ship. Cabin stewards, waiters, bar stewards, junior galley personnel, cleaners and laundry workers constitute crew, although many other hotel department members fall into the category of ship's staff.

The **deck department** is responsible for navigation, safety and the structural maintenance of the vessel. In charge of this department is the **Captain** – who, as

Master, also has overall command of the ship. The second-in-command is the **Staff Captain**, followed by the **Chief Officer** and deck officers. The bosun, able seamen (ABs) and ordinary seamen constitute the deck department crew. Affiliated to the deck department are the **communications division** (under the **Chief Radio Officer**) and the **security division** (under the **Chief Security Officer**).

The **engine department** is responsible for the maintenance and operation of the engines, electrical and technical facilities. In charge is the **Chief Engineer**, assisted by the **Staff Chief Engineer**, engineering and electrical officers. The oilers, motormen and technical ratings (non-officers) constitute the crew of this department.

By far the largest sector of a passenger ship is the **hotel department**, encompassing all aspects of passenger services, finance, catering, housekeeping and entertainment. In charge of this department is the **Hotel Manager**, supported by the following officers and their respective personnel: the **Purser** – responsible for finance, documentation, cabin allocation and passenger information; the **Cruise Director** – responsible for entertainment, social activities and events, daily programming and, possibly, shore excursions; the **Executive Chef** – responsible for the galley and all areas of food preparation; the **Food and Beverage Manager** – responsible for the catering service and supplies, assisted by the Restaurant Manager/maître d'hôtel; the **Bars Manager** – responsible for the bar service and supplies; the **Chief Steward** – responsible for the public rooms (and, on some ships, room service); and the **Housekeeper** – responsible for the room service and laundry, assisted by the **Laundry Master**.

The smallest division of most ships is the **medical department** under the charge of the **Principal Medical Officer**. The PMO is responsible for the hospital and all medical issues and supplies relating to both passengers and the ship's company. They may be assisted by other medical officers (doctors, nurses) and medical crew members or petty officers, such as orderlies and dispensers.

Above: *Room service – courtesy of a cabin steward.* **Opposite**: *Full concentration on the bridge of the* RMS St Helena *as her navigation officers bring her into port.*

YOUR CABIN STEWARD

For the duration of your cruise you will be allocated the services of a cabin steward or stewardess. They are responsible for **cleaning** the cabin, making the beds and replenishing supplies of soap, towels, tissues, toilet paper and other toiletry items. They will also deliver your **room-service** breakfast, your minibar requests and buckets of ice, and take your **washing** to the laundry.

Headline Acts

As a rule of thumb, the bigger the ship, the better the entertainment programme. Leading the way in offering impressive, hi-tech production shows are Carnival, Princess and Crystal Cruises.

Video Nasties

Due to copyright regulations, the videoing of shows and on-board performances is often prohibited. An announcement to this effect is generally made before a show. Taking footage of a band or other aspect of 'life aboard' is, however, generally acceptable.

Entertainment and Activities

Shipboard entertainment has come a long way since the days of the Purser's amateur variety show. Many vessels now boast **extensive entertainment programmes** featuring elaborate nightly shows, discos, karaoke, theme evenings, guest lecturers, live bands and professional entertainers. **Facilities** are also increasingly impressive, with full-scale, hi-tech **theatres**, **lecture halls** and **cinemas** showing the latest blockbuster movies. On a mainstream cruise ship you could attend a celebrity lecture in the morning, a dance class in the afternoon, enjoy a classical recital before dinner, listen to a big band, watch a professional show then dance the night away in the disco. Where could you do all that in a single venue back home, especially when it's all thrown in with the price of your accommodation?

The evening's entertainment is generally complimented by a programme of **daytime** activities, particularly on days at sea. Bingo, horse-racing (using wooden horses and dice!), game shows, pool games, quizzes, contests and get-togethers are often orgainized by a team of out-going cruise staff, some of whom may double as entertainers in the evening.

Visiting **experts**, **celebrities** and **lecturers** also frequently feature in shipboard entertainment programmes, particularly on themed cruises. The most popular subjects

Below: *Glitzy and flamboyant entertainment on* Carnival Fascination.

Left: *Relaxing in* Star Princess*'s on-deck jacuzzis.*

are Contract Bridge, Arts and Crafts, Handwriting Analysis, Self-improvement, Portraits and Caricatures, Ballroom Dancing, Fashion, Finance, Astrology and all forms of Fortune-Telling.

Of course, should you prefer a quiet night in, your choice of **in-cabin television** viewing will probably include local and/or satellite TV, a news channel, ship's channel (with daily programme updates, topical information and, sometimes, interviews with passengers or members of the ship's company) and one or two movies. Larger ships may even employ a television station manager and staff, while up-scale smaller vessels may operate an impressive **video lending service** for in-cabin viewing.

Health and Fitness

In keeping with modern health trends, most cruise ships offer sports and fitness facilities and an increasing number of vessels now boast well-equipped

SPORTS STARS

NORWEGIAN CRUISE LINE (NCL) offers **sporting themed cruises** and excellent sports facilities that include a **basketball** court on its flagship, the *Norway*. The *Royal Viking Sun* has its own **croquet lawn** while the latest ROYAL CARIBBEAN ships even boast an **18-hole golf course**. Several smaller vessels (notably, the ships of SEABOURN, WINDSTAR and CUNARD'S *Sea Goddess* I and II) incorporate a **water-sports platform** with appropriate facilities, while FRED OLSEN LINE has cleverly transformed the former-ferry stern of the *Black Prince* into its own retractable **Marina Park**, complete with sailing, water-skiing and windsurfing amenities.

Right: *Life aboard a cruise ship isn't all about taking it easy – here passengers enjoy a mid-ocean game of volleyball.*

gymnasiums and **spas**, comparable to top private health clubs on land. In fact, such is the emphasis placed upon health and fitness in modern ship design that spas commonly occupy a prime location high at the front of the ship, affording panoramic views as well as hi-tech equipment.

While features such as **swimming pools** are almost standard on cruise ships these days, the range of sports facilities and services found on some of the modern vessels can be as unexpected as it is surprising, with such things as **jogging tracks**, **golf driving ranges** or **putting greens**, **aerobics classes**, **saunas** and **giant chess boards** found on different vessels. **Aerobics classes**, **table-tennis** and other sporting **tournaments** and **skeet/clay pigeon shooting** may be organized as part of the shipboard programme.

While basic workout equipment may be unsupervised, those vessels with well-equipped gymnasiums invariably employ **qualified sports instructors** to offer supervision and instruction. For a fee, these professionals can also assist with personal training programmes and body fat analysis.

In addition, most mainstream cruise ships provide **hairdressing** and **beauty services** (e.g. facials, manicures and make-overs) and many have extensive facilities with a large salon and health massage rooms. Often these are operated by the spa concessionaire and may be located within the spa itself.

Health and Fitness Cost-Cutter's Tips

Deck games and general fitness facilities (pool, jogging track, gymnasium etc.) are usually **free**, but expect to be charged extra for **personal treatments** provided by the concessionary spa or beauty salon. These include hairdressing services, manicures, facials, massages, personal training programmes, body fat analysis and hydrotherapy treatments. You can keep costs down by **checking the price** of treatments and services before making your appointment and guarding against being cajoled into buying additional 'take home' items such as creams, gels or lotions.

Shipboard Gambling

In former days gambling aboard cruise ships amounted to little more than a game of bingo or the Purser's version of the Kentucky Derby. Now, however, gambling is one of the cruise industry's biggest money-spinners, with the casinos of many modern vessels occupying a substantial proportion of a major deck. Indeed, such is the demand for shipboard gambling that certain privately owned or chartered vessels – sailing, most notably, out of Singapore – are marketed almost exclusively as floating casinos.

Some of the most impressive casinos at sea can be found on the larger, newer ships of CELEBRITY, CARNIVAL, PRINCESS and ROYAL CARIBBEAN cruise lines. Such gambling palaces can easily rival large shore-side casinos with **blackjack tables**, several **roulette** and **craps** tables, 40 or 50 **poker machines** and hundreds of **slot machines**. As an inspiration, gamblers may also be interested to learn that, in 1994, a single jackpot of over $1 million was paid out aboard CARNIVAL'S *Jubilee*. Although an increasing number of cruise lines operate their own casinos, others are managed by concessionaires such as **Casinos Austria** or **London Clubs**. The beautiful Romanesque gambling rooms aboard the ships of CRYSTAL CRUISES are, appropriately, operated by **Caesars Palace at Sea**.

Keen gamblers should opt for itineraries that include the maximum time **at sea** as, along with duty-free shops, shipboard casinos are not permitted to open when the vessel is in port.

GAMBLING TIPS

In order that the cost of your gambling pleasure doesn't spoil your cruise, it is a good idea to decide on a **daily 'flutter budget'** and stick to it – even if the slot you've been feeding looks set to pay out on the very next coin!

Below: *When the chips are down – living it up at the on-board casino.*

TIPS FOR HONEYMOONERS

• Avoid ships where the **age range** is greatly different from your own – such as cruises geared to the family or seniors market.
• Specify at the time of booking if you require a **double bed**. Some cabins only have separate twin berths.
• Also indicate if you would prefer to be at a **table for two** in the restaurant.
• Avoid itineraries noted for **rough seas**. *Mal de mer* is not conducive to romance.
• As honeymooners, you could be eligible for free champagne or gifts. Ask when you book.

Shipboard Weddings and Honeymoons

Contrary to common belief, the Captain is not empowered to conduct marriages aboard – or at least any attachment legally recognized beyond the duration of the cruise. Shipboard weddings are, however, very much in vogue, with a shore-based minister or priest brought on to conduct the ceremony while the vessel is in port.

Complete **wedding packages** that include a shipboard ceremony (with an officiate provided either by the participants or the cruise line) and an inclusive cruise honeymoon are offered by AMERICAN HAWAII, CARNIVAL, CELEBRITY, COMMODORE, HOLLAND AMERICA, NCL, PRINCESS, ROYAL CARIBBEAN and WINDJAMMER BAREFOOT CRUISES.

Dress Codes

Whether lauded or maligned, adhered to or ignored, the evening dress code is an integral and traditional feature of taking a cruise. While the **cost** of the cruise can be an indicator of the degree of formality you can expect, the **style** of the cruise should also be taken into account. Most **coastal**, **river**, **explorer** and **sail ships** tend to be casual, irrespective of their price tag, while **deluxe yacht-like vessels** are synonymous with understated elegance rather than glitz. In very general terms, ships catering to **North American** or **Australian** passengers tend to be more casual than those catering to Europeans; **Japanese** ships are among the dressiest of the Asian market; and particularly dazzling evening wear can be seen on ships with a **Latin American** clientele.

Long gowns and dinner suits or tuxedos are perfectly appropriate for the Captain's party on a prestige liner, but they are likely to be out of place on a ship catering specifically to families. On the other hand, a short-sleeved shirt and jeans could never pass for formal wear on any mainstream vessel. If in doubt, look at the cruise brochure and pack clothes you feel are in keeping with those of the passengers depicted.

Dress codes traditionally fall into the following categories: **Formal**, which would indicate a dinner jacket

DRESS AND FANCY DRESS

There may be a 'themed' casual evening planned during your cruise – for example a Caribbean or Country and Western night – to which you may want to wear an appropriate outfit. COSTA CRUISES' Toga Night is one of the best-organized theme evenings, with sheets and laurel wreaths keenly sported by last-night passengers who have already packed most of their clothes.

Left: *The relaxed, romantic ambience of a sailing cruise with* WINDJAMMER BAREFOOT CRUISES.

(tuxedo) or suit (preferably dark) for men and an evening gown or cocktail dress for ladies; **Informal**, a suit or jacket/blazer and tie for men and a dress, separates or trouser (pant) suit for ladies; and **Casual**, when jacket and tie is not required for men, and slacks or separates are suitable for ladies.

Of course, the dress code is only a guide and nobody is going to refuse to serve you if you choose not to comply. For many passengers, however, sparkling formal nights are part of cruising's glamorous image and give their holiday a sense of occasion.

On-Board Dining

Dining should be a highlight of your cruise, and while styles and standards vary enormously, most cruise ships try hard to look after you in this department. On mainstream cruise lines you will find waiter-service or self-service buffet options for **breakfast** and **lunch**, waiter-service **dinner** and various buffet-style **snacks** available around the clock. The buffets are usually extensive and attractively presented, often featuring impressive ice sculptures and vegetable carvings. Indeed, it sometimes seems that more guests attend the spectacular Gala Buffet to photograph the whole thing than to eat it!

Special Diets

Most lines offer **vegetarian** options on their menu, together with dishes for the health-conscious, **diabetic** desserts and low-salt/fat/sodium dishes. For specific dietary requests, check with your cruise line at the time of booking. Most ships can accommodate special diets – from **kosher** to **additive-free** – providing adequate advance notice is given.

A Weight-Watchers' Guide to On-Board Eating

07:00 **Room Service**: An orange juice and croissant (for starters).
08:00 **Breakfast**: Full American/English/Continental-style, either waiter service in the restaurant or alfresco at the self-service buffet on deck (to set you up for the rest of the day).
11:00 **Elevenses** in the lounge or traditional hot bouillon on deck (just to keep you going).
13:00 **Lunch**: Either full à la carte in the restaurant or something light (or maybe not!) at the deck buffet.
16:00 **Afternoon Tea**: Just one or two sandwiches, cakes and biscuits (but only to fill the gap).
20:00 **Dinner**: Five courses plus coffee (so as not to offend the chef).
24:00 **Midnight Buffet**: Go along 'just to look' (everyone *else* does!).

The **evening meal** tends to be the most structured with waiter service and a dinner menu offering appetizers, soups, salads, three or four entrées (main courses), a selection of desserts, cheese board and coffee. Many of the larger ships also offer **fast-food** alternatives such as 24-hour pizzerias, snack bars, burger stands and popcorn carts, together with restaurants offering different types of cuisine (such as Chinese, Japanese, or Italian-style). And in case you get peckish in between, you can always order **room service**.

The standards of cuisine are generally reflected in the **price** of your cruise, but the **nationality** of the chefs, officers and crew may have a great bearing on the overall culinary style and choice of dishes. For example, **Greek** specialities are an integral part of Royal Olympic's menu; a **Chinese** or **Japanese** restaurant are among the dining options offered by Crystal Cruises; and Costa's ships have – literally – an **Italian** flavour, including *gelato* carts and all-day pizzerias. The nationality of the passengers may also influence the menu (ships catering to the German market, for example, may place a greater emphasis on breads and cold meats).

Right: *A lavish Norwegian cold buffet.*

Above: *A special Fijian seafood platter – the perfect dish for an island-hopping South Seas cruise.*

Which Sitting?

Most of the small yacht-like vessels and a few large-ship restaurants at the deluxe end of the scale offer the attraction of **open sitting** dining – that is, you may request a table *with whom* you like, *where* you like, *when* you like (within the restaurant opening hours). In a similar vein, but with diners keeping to an allocated table, some ships are able to offer **single sitting** dining. The vast majority of cruise ships, however, because of the number of passengers, are obliged to offer a more structured dining arrangement – namely **two restaurant sittings**. The time of your sitting applies to all restaurant meals (breakfast, lunch and dinner), but because many guests select self-service buffet alternatives for breakfast and lunch, it is the preferred dinner time that is often the deciding factor. **First sitting** dinner normally commences between 18:00 and 18:30, **second sitting** between 20:00 and 20:30 and the restaurant doors normally close 15 minutes after the start of service. The **first** sitting is normally more attractive to those travelling with young children and passengers who prefer not to linger over dinner. The **second** sitting is preferred by those who intend hosting or attending cocktail parties, who prefer to linger over their meal, or who habitually dine later.

Having established your sitting, you may wish to request a particular **table** – near the window, smoking/non-smoking, or for a specific number of people. Taking into account that tables for two (and singles) are rare, it is a good idea to request a table for six to eight people – especially as it is standard practice to keep the same dining partners for the duration of your cruise. Tables for four can be a bit too intimate, particularly if you don't click with your companions, while tables for 10 can be a little too large for everyone to join in a conversation.

Dinner Sittings and Cocktail Parties

If you are hoping to join in fully with the social side of a cruise, it is worth remembering that **first-sitting diners** generally lose out in the cocktail party stakes. As an example, the Captain's Welcome Party for first-sitting guests on the Gala Night is usually scheduled so early that those returning from excursions barely have time to change. **Ships' officers** are also far more likely to be in attendance at the second sitting cocktail party and to host a table at the second sitting dinner.

Invitations to an Officer's Table

During a cruise, you may be invited to join a senior officer's table. Some ships invite guests to dine with officers on a **one-off** or **rota** basis, while other vessels may seat diners with a designated officer for the **duration** of the cruise. If, for whatever reason, you wish to **decline** an invitation to an officer's table, be sure to inform the maître d' (you don't *need* to give your reason – unlike the lady who declined the Captain's table by declaring: 'I didn't pay all this money to come on a cruise, only to eat with the crew'!).

If you have definite dining preferences, be sure to advise your cruise line at the time of **booking**. To confirm (or reconfirm) your sitting or make specific table requests, see the maître d' as soon as possible after you embark and if you are unhappy with your allocated table or sitting, make this known as early as possible in the cruise. The same applies if, after your first meal together, you realise that you and your new table companions are never going to hit it off. Wherever possible the maître d' will re-accommodate you, subject to space availability.

Drinks

Beverages and soft drinks are not always included in the price of a cruise and these items could add considerable weight to your bill. Most ships offer **free tea and coffee** (sometimes round-the-clock), although you are likely to be charged for espressos and cappuccinos. **Bottled water** is often free, together with the **fruit juices** at breakfast/lunch buffets, but **soft drinks** ordered at the bar will probably be charged.

With the exception of situations where you are offered a drink at a private party or an official event (such as the Captain's Reception or the Singles Mingle), expect all **alcoholic drinks** to be charged. Certain deluxe vessels have an all-inclusive drinks policy, but such costs are effectively covered by the premium price-tag. A good tip to remember is that unless specifically outlawed in the small print of your cruise brochure, consider buying bottles of Duty Free in your ports-of-call for pre-dinner cabin parties. Consuming your own drinks in the public lounges and deck areas is, of course, as unacceptable as taking your own drinks to the local pub, but shoreside purchases of regional wine may be opened at dinner, subject to a corkage fee.

Gratuities

Policies on tipping crew members such as your waiter/waitress and cabin steward differ from ship to ship, but for many cruise passengers, gratuities can be the costliest

Left: *Dining at an officer's table on the up-market* CRYSTAL *line.*

of their on-board extras. **Per person per day** (PPPD) guidelines are usually stated in the ship's brochure and repeated during the cruise director's disembarkation briefing, but uncertainties and ambiguities inevitably arise.

Some lines have adopted strict no tipping policies and others include gratuities in the price of the cruise, but the vast majority give 'recommendations' as to how much you should tuck into those little envelopes that miraculously appear in your cabin on the last day. In addition to their **cabin steward**, their **waiter** and their **busboy**, passengers may also want to tip the **maître d'** and **spa/beauty salon**, **casino and bar staff**, and, on smaller vessels, perhaps even the **cruise director** and **members of the cruise staff**. If you participate in organized shore excursions, you may also wish to tip your **tour guides** and **drivers**. Note that most cruise lines automatically add **15 per cent service charge** onto bar bills. The policy on **Greek** ships or those with an **open sitting** is that restaurant tips are usually pooled.

Whenever possible, give your gratuity **directly to the person** you wish to tip. If you prefer the convenience of signing tips on your **shipboard account** (as some lines encourage), bear in mind that staff members are likely to remain unaware of the different sources of the lump-sum gratuity they receive.

TIPPING GUIDELINES

- Never take tipping levels recommended by cruise lines to be an indication of the **quality of service**. In fact, those lines that discourage gratuities are frequently among the service leaders.
- Presuming you are satisfied with the level of service, **don't skimp** on gratuities. Many cruise employees rely heavily on tips to make up their income.
- **Budget-conscious** passengers should minimize the number of situations where tipping may be expected rather than skimping on the tips themselves.
- Take tips into account when calculating the total cost of your cruise. If there is no mention of gratuities in the line's publicity, don't presume they are not expected.

SEA SICKNESS REMEDIES

- **Wrist bands** work by applying pressure to the acupressure points. These should be worn continuously while sailing and cause no known side effects.
- Non-prescription **sea sickness pills** (such as Dramamine) should be taken two hours prior to sailing and may cause drowsiness.
- Anti-sea sickness **injections** can be administered by the ship's medical staff for more immediate relief of symptoms. They may also cause drowsiness.
- **Homeopathic** remedies often include root ginger – a natural antidote with no known side effects.

Prevention, however, is always better than the cure:

- Avoid **rich**, **fatty foods**. If you start feeling queasy, eat dry, salted **crackers**.
- **Avoid smoke-filled atmospheres** – if possible, head for the open decks and fill up with **fresh air**.
- Concentrate on the **horizon** (*not* the waves!).

Health and Safety At Sea

Seasickness

It can be a great disappointment for shipboard passengers when their dream holiday is blighted by seasickness. Various remedies exist to combat this complaint, although none are guaranteed to work and different people tend to find that different cures work best for them.

Of course, the risk of sea sickness can be diminished with the help of a little **forward planning**. Potential sufferers should select an **inside** cabin towards the **middle** of a **lower** deck, choose a **larger** ship and/or one with a **deep draft**, and select an itinerary noted for **calm waters** (such as Alaska's Inside Passage), avoiding regions with notoriously strong currents (such as the Bay of Biscay, Bay of Bengal or Bering Strait) or where seas converge (such as the Cape of Good Hope or Cape Horn).

Charges for Medical Services

Unless otherwise stated in your brochure, expect to be charged for any medical services that you require during your cruise. You will, of course, be given a receipt for **insurance claims**, but the cost of minor treatments is likely to be within the policy's excess figure and therefore not eligible for reimbursement.

Bear in mind that, whatever the complaint, you will be charged a **consultancy fee** (usually US$15) if you visit the doctor, so avoid the medical centre for minor ailments. The on-board shop will probably stock basic remedies for things such as a stuffy nose or heat rash. If you do need to see the doctor, try and go during **surgery hours**. An hefty additional call-out fee may be charged if the doctor has to visit your cabin.

Shipboard Security

In keeping with other forms of transportation in today's modern world, cruise ships have become increasingly security-conscious, with larger vessels even contracting specialist firms to supply round-the-clock security personnel. You are likely to find at least one person on security duty at the **gangway** whenever the ship is in port, and you will be expected to produce your **boarding card** (your shipboard identification) when coming to and from the ship.

While this undoubtedly affords a certain peace of mind, the downside is that the associated '**No Visitors' policy** can sometimes be restrictive to passengers. Do not, for example, expect friends or family members to be allowed aboard on embarkation day to see you off. Access can also be difficult for personal visitors in your ports of call, although requests may be considered subject to adequate notice – ask at the purser's desk.

Going Ashore

For many people, the highlight of their cruise is not the ship or being at sea but the opportunity to visit various ports and, perhaps, several different countries during the course of their vacation. No other form of holiday allows such comfortable, hassle-free travel to as many different places in a limited space of time.

In order to fully enjoy your time in each port, however, it is important to be aware of both the attractions and the

Cruising Health and Safety Tips

- **Fire** is a serious hazard, so be aware of the risks. Lit cigarettes, for example, should not be thrown overboard as they could easily blow back onto the ship.
- Don't leave **breakable objects** on surfaces where they could easily slide off with the motion of the ship.
- Avoid eating **salads** and **poorly cooked food** when ashore in areas noted for food risks.
- Shipboard **tap water** is usually quite safe to drink, but its taste is often impaired by chlorine. **Bottled water** should be available from your cabin steward, in the restaurant or in the bar.
- **Sunburn** – especially in tropical regions – ruins as many shipboard holidays as sea sickness.

Left: *Ashore for a shopping spree on St Thomas in the US Virgin Islands.*

SAFE ASHORE

When sightseeing or wandering around the streets of a foreign port, take the following precautions.

- **Blend in** as much as possible. Dress conservatively and don't flaunt expensive-looking jewellery, videos or cameras.
- Women, in particular, may be **hassled** in certain countries – the best reaction is usually no reaction. Even in the face of unprovoked aggression, both sexes should **avoid confrontations** with locals.
- Be sure not to amble too far **off the beaten track** in places with high-crime rates (your cruise director can advise you). In certain ports it may be advisable not to walk at all – take taxis.

problems that may await. Some ports are more interesting than others, some are more expensive, and some are more dangerous.

Shoreside Survival

It is always wise to get a low-down on the place you are visiting **before** you step down the gangway. Do a little **background reading** and attend the **briefings** given by the cruise director and shore excursion manager. Have in your mind what you would like to see or do and ask their advice on the best way to achieve this.

Once you step ashore, you should follow a few obvious guidelines to help you **stay safe** (*see* Box). In general, respect local customs and traditions (such as taking off shoes in religious places where appropriate). Be aware that becoming drunk and disorderly or getting into a brush with the law can have more serious repercussions than back home, while casual sexual encounters (particularly with prostitutes) or anything connected with the trafficking of drugs should definitely be avoided.

Cruise ships are, on the whole, much safer than hotels, so you can leave **valuables** aboard and there is no

Right: *A civic welcome awaits the passengers of the* Polariys *on the quayside of Rorvik in Norway.*

Left: *The* Island Princess *is able to take her passengers right into the heart of historic Venice.*

need to carry large amounts of cash. Try not to carry your cash and credit cards together and never count wads of money in public. Although **foreign currencies** (especially US dollars) are widely accepted in international tourist areas, this should never be presumed, and even if they are prices quoted in foreign currencies are often relatively high. **Credit cards** are still an unfamiliar form of payment in the world's poorest countries and, even when accepted, the authorization process can be painfully slow.

It is a good idea to write the **name of your ship**, together with the **name of the harbour** (and, if applicable, the pier number) to show to taxi drivers who do not speak your language. Even better, write these details on the back of a postcard depicting your vessel. Be sure to note the **'All Aboard' time** when you leave your vessel and allow yourself enough time to get back, taking traffic conditions into account. If you are heading off independently,

Avoiding Rip-Offs

Don't be an easy victim when you are ashore.

- Take a **pocket calculator** with you to work out exchange rates and prices.
- Be wary of **scams** – bottles of spirits or perfume sold in the street could contain nothing more than tea or water. Other scams try to take advantage of cruise ship passengers in particular – be suspicious if:
- Your tour guide rushes you through places of interest, only to spend over an hour at a souvenir shop.
- Your taxi driver insists on taking you to a particular shop or restaurant even though you requested to go somewhere else.
- The 'officially-recommended' retail outlets sell comparable items to those of competing shops – but at a far higher price!

it is worth taking the contact details of the **port agent** with you, in case you are delayed and miss the ship's departure.

Organized Excursions

Many ships have a **shore excursion desk** manned by a shore excursion manager and staff, which offers a selection of optional tours throughout your cruise. Unless clearly stated otherwise, expect to pay for all organized shore excursions. If you are watching your budget, be **selective** about which excursions, if any, you take. One truly memorable excursion, such as a helicopter or adventure trip, may be worthy of inclusion over several mediocre coach tours. Local transportation often provides a cheaper option and you may be able to stroll independently to the major sights.

However, there are a number of distinct advantages to taking organized trips. For example, you are usually covered by the **ship's insurance** if you incur an accident or injury during an organized tour. If you go off independently, you are not. There is also more **safety**, as well as companionship, in numbers, which might be particularly attractive to single or elderly passengers. If an official ship's tour is **late** arriving back at the pier, the vessel will wait as long as possible before sailing. In contrast, the ship is unlikely to wait for you if you go ashore independently – and you would be personally responsible for any costs or arrangements incurred in rejoining the vessel.

Tips on Booking Shore Excursions

- If you are keen to do a particular tour, **book early**, as places may be limited.
- Be **selective**. A shore excursion is usually offered in almost every port – whether there is anything worth visiting or not.
- **Plan ahead**. Try putting as much **variety** into your sightseeing programme as possible.
- Ask the **shore excursion staff** for their advice. They are there to provide information as well as sell tours.

Left: *Colourful shoreside entertainment in Sumbawa in Indonesia.*
Opposite: *When you're ashore, it's always good to know the way home – here the* CARNIVAL *livery can be made out among the houses of Nassau in the Bahamas.*

Taking into account the limitations of developing countries, the **transportation** for the organized tours is likely to be of a reasonable standard and your guide well-informed and able to speak your language. If you venture off alone, the standards of local modes of transport and the skills of private drivers and guides cannot be guaranteed. Also worth considering are that **entrance fees**, which can add up if you visit the same places independently, are included in the price of your tour, and that certain types of excursions (specific adventure trips, private theatrical performances etc.) may be available **only** through the ship's shore excursion office.

On the other hand, **independent** travel can be a lot more exciting. You are able to escape the tourist traps and avoid restaurants and beaches packed with fellow passengers. Local transportation is likely to be cheaper and presuming you feel comfortable driving in your given destination, **renting cars** and **mopeds** can be a fun way to get around. You will not be restricted by a sightseeing schedule, so you can choose where to go and for how long. Neither are you rushed through your personal highlight only to spend an hour waiting for fellow passengers at a less interesting location or shopping stop. You are much more likely to discover a simple back street taverna frequented by local residents which gives you a much better taste of the 'real' destination.

AT THE END . . .

The last day of your cruise will doubtless come about all too soon. When it approaches, there are a few useful things to remember:

- Leave out **something to wear** on disembarkation morning – a surprising number of passengers pack all their shoes and daytime clothes.
- Hand in **gratuity envelopes** and **questionnaires** before disembarkation morning. It is best to tip crew members the day before disembarkation, as there is no guarantee you will see them on the final morning.
- **Luggage** (other than hand luggage) should be labelled and placed outside your cabin door the night prior to disembarkation.
- Check **meal hours**. Breakfast service may be rescheduled and room service unavailable on disembarkation morning.
- Don't **mill around** the main reception area or the gangway as it may be some time before you are able to get off.

4
Special Interest Cruising

Cruising has an enviable reputation as a style of holiday which has always appealed to a wide range of people. In particular, cruise lines often make special efforts to attract single, disabled and elderly passengers, as well as family groups and those keen to pursue their particular interests in subjects such as wildlife, history, music and sport. Discovering the range of options available can open an exciting array of holiday opportunities for these groups.

Singles-Friendly Cruise Lines

Some companies are noticeably more tuned-in to the requirements of solo travellers than others. Hebridean Island Cruises, World Explorer Cruises and Ivaran Lines all offer supplement-free cruising for singles. Orient Lines, while normally charging 25 per cent, waives surcharges altogether during its low season and various other cruise lines also waive or reduce surcharges, subject to supply and demand. Commodore Cruise Line also offers a regular singles theme cruise.

Cruising for Singles

Each year, more than a million solo travellers take a cruise – and with good reason. Cruising offers ready-made companionship, but enough space to enjoy one's own company as well as that of others. It is a basically crime-free environment and provides safety in numbers when venturing ashore, and it offers an integrated social scene without the alienation and hassles of unwanted attention that women, in particular, might otherwise experience. Of course if the attention is *not* unwanted, then cruising can also provide the perfect backdrop for romance.

Seasoned single passengers are found on ships of all shapes and sizes, and especially on **longer**, **more expensive** cruises. Young solo first-timers are more likely to 'test the water' on three to four-day '**party**' **cruises** out of Florida or Piraeus (the port for Athens), while Carnival Cruise Lines caters to more young singles than any other line – which is not surprising as it also carries more passengers than any other line.

Opposite: *You're never too old to learn the ropes.*

Information for Cruising Singles

• *The Single Traveler* is an American newsletter that publishes information on special deals for singles on cruises (and other holidays). For more details contact 2849 West Dundee Rd, No. 118, Northbrook, IL 60062, USA. Tel: (+1) 708-272-6788.

• In the USA, some cruise agencies – such as **Singleworld** and **Travel Companion Exchange** – also provide cabin matches for singles as part of their booking service.

Gentleman Hosts

Taking into account the fact that on most cruises the number of single ladies tends to far outweigh the number of single men, companies such as Cunard, Crystal, Celebrity, Ivaran, Norwegian (NCL), Orient, Delta Queen Steamboat Co. and Holland America Line employ gentleman hosts to partner passengers at bridge games, act as escorts and – especially – whisk female passengers around the dance floor every night.

The Singles' Mingle

On any cruise there will usually be at least one cocktail party or get-together for solo passengers scheduled fairly early in the cruise. This is not a lonely hearts club, but rather a chance to get to know and recognize your fellow travellers and the members of the social staff who host the event. If your hosts are inventive and the guests interesting, there is no reason why this should not develop into a lively and memorable occasion.

Single Supplements

As with land-based hotel accommodation, cabin prices are generally based on two people sharing and single guests occupying double rooms are therefore charged an addition to the standard rate. This figure varies from company to company (check the brochures) but is usually 50 per cent on top of the standard per person tariff and as much as double for a high grade suite. This does leave many solo travellers feeling they are, literally, paying for their independence.

In general, single travellers with a taste for adventure are well-catered for on **unusual, destination-orientated** or **explorer** cruises. In addition, some **passenger-cargo** ships such as Ivaran Line's *Americana* provide supplement-free cruising and gentlemen hosts, and allocate over a third of its cabins to single occupancy. For more mainstream cruising, **shop around** for a good deal – remember that cruise lines would often prefer to make a last-minute special deal on a double cabin to a single person than leave it unoccupied, so if you are footloose and flexible, you could strike it lucky.

If you want to **avoid paying** a single supplement, however, it's worth knowing some of the options.

• **Double-up**. If you don't mind sharing, this option at least solves the financial dilemma and can provide ready-made companionship. The obvious choice of cabin-mate would be a **friend** or **relative**, but you can let the cruise line play matchmaker. Opt for a '**guaranteed share' cabin** and the cruise line will try and place you with a compatible person of the same sex, taking into

account factors such as age, nationality and smoking preferences. This, of course, is always a gamble, but if the ship isn't full or the line doesn't come up with a match for you, you could end up with the cabin to yourself and at no extra charge. This is more likely to occur on repositioning and low season cruises.

- **Go for a guaranteed singles rate**. This means you pay a set price for guaranteed single occupancy of a double cabin, but you won't know which cabin you have been allocated until you actually board the ship. Although you will probably be charged no more than the lowest end of the double-occupancy scale and should therefore expect inside accommodation, you could be in for a pleasant surprise, especially in low season.
- **Book a single cabin**. There is no supplement payable on single occupancy cabins, but that does not mean to say it is necessarily a less expensive option. You are, of course, assured of private accommodation, but be aware that it could also be on the small side and unusually shaped or located. Bear in mind, too, that a single cabin means a single bed.

By far the most single cabins are found aboard P&O's *Oriana* and CUNARD's *Queen Elizabeth 2* (with 112 and

Above: *WINDJAMMER BAREFOOT CRUISES offers popular singles-only cruises in the Caribbean.*

SAILING SINGLES

Enthusiasts of tall ships and sail-powered cruising may be attracted to the ships of WINDJAMMER BAREFOOT CRUISES, which offers singles-only trips with a good male/female balance and age mix about four times a year.

Above: *Bar service on the high-profile P&O ship* Oriana, *a well-established choice for cruising singles.*

116 single cabins respectively). Other cruise ships offering a reasonable range of purpose-built single accommodation include: *Americana, Black Prince, Europa, Fascination, Funchal, Star Aquarius, Norway, Saga Rose, Victoria* and *Vistafjord.*

- **Rough it**. Sometimes cruise lines are prepared to waive their single supplement if you accept one of their 'less desirable' cabins – i.e. next to a busy pantry, with a porthole instead of a window or an inside berth with fold-up bunk beds. If you opt for the latter, you may find yourself in reasonably sized accommodation and the unoccupied bunks, when unfolded from the wall, provide excellent 'shelves' for extra storage.

Shipboard Romance

As screen titles such as *The Love Boat, One Way Passage, An Affair to Remember* and *Gentlemen Prefer Blondes* testify, cruising has always been synonymous with romance. While all ships can be romantic in different ways, it is the bigger vessels that are especially likely to afford the most opportunities for budding romances. On the whole, smaller yacht-like ships will tend to attract couples.

Despite the romantic image of cruising, however, it is important not to set expectations too high. Too many lonely hearts place undue emphasis on cruising's 'Loveboat' associations and are disappointed when a romance fails to materialize. The best potential meeting places on board are the hot tub, the golf driving range, the gymnasium, dance classes and special interest activities. Themed cruises, where participants share a common link, can also provide an excellent starting block for romance.

Gay Cruises

Single homosexual or lesbian travellers might be interested to know that specialist travel companies – such as US-based **R.S.V.P. Cruises** and **Olivia Cruises** (for women) – market exclusively gay charters. Advertisements for gay cruises can also be found in appropriate international newspapers and magazines.

Cruising for Families

Taking a cruise on a family-orientated ship is one of the best options available to parents wishing to include the kids in an all-inclusive holiday abroad. Ships provide an encapsulated environment where children can participate in a number of different supervised activities and teenagers have the freedom to do their own thing. In turn, parents can enjoy moments of family togetherness, interspersed with valuable time to themselves.

Single parents may appreciate the feeling of space and ready-made companionship (both for them and their children) that is afforded by a family-style ship. Cruising is also an excellent way of travelling with other family members of mixed age-groups (including **grandparents**) as everyone is free to engage in individual activities and still meet up at mealtimes or to go ashore.

Sharing with Children

Lines that target the family market commonly allow up to two children to travel free (or at a substantial discount) if they share a cabin with two full-fare paying adults. If flights and port taxes are included, this can amount to a good saving, but if they are not, it may be worth paying a little more for the extra privacy of two adjacent cabins. If you are travelling with teenagers, and the cost is not too prohibitive, the freedom of separate accommodation would probably benefit all concerned.

Activities for Children

While you will find that most cruise lines profess to offer 'something for all the family', only those that seriously market to this sector will provide extensive children's facilities and programmes. Some ships that are generally adult-only may employ seasonal childrens' staff during school holiday periods, but do double-check when you book that a childrens' programme exists during the time you intend to travel.

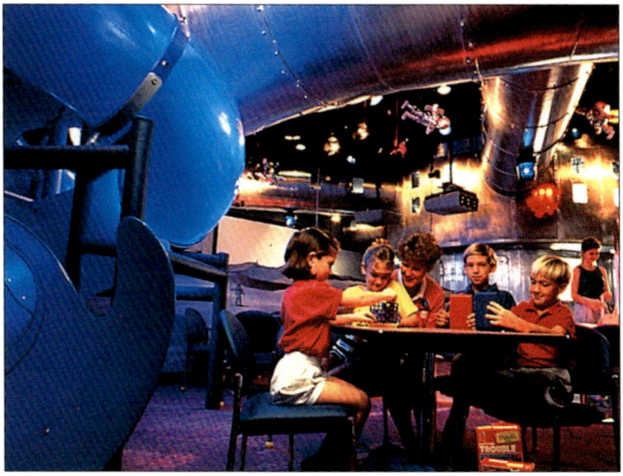

Below: *The hi-tech Kids Konnection games room on* Nordic Empress.

Cartoon Cruises

With the first of its megaships, *Disney Magic*, launched in 1988, Disney Cruise Lines are undoubtedly destined to become a major competitor in the family cruising marketplace and sure to include many favourite cartoon characters to rival those already running around the decks of other lines (Woody Woodpecker is NCL'S Universal Studios star while Hannah-Barbera's Yogi Bear frolics aboard the Premier fleet).

Meal Times

On most ships adults will be expected to eat with their offspring at the **early sitting** (where there are two sittings) for the evening meal, although lines such as P&O and Carnival do give parents a break with separate junior dinner arrangements.

Right: *Video games for youngsters who find the progress of a cruise ship a bit too sedate.*

On ships that encourage young children you should find baby foods and care items, children's menus, high chairs and cots are readily available. Such vessels may also provide extensive play areas, video game arcades, teens' discos and separate junior swimming pools. Some of the best children's facilities afloat (including an impressive video arcade) can be found aboard Star Cruise's Singapore-based ship, *Star Aquarius*. Other forerunners of family-oriented cruising include Airtours, American Hawaii, Carnival, Celebrity, Commodore, Premier, Norwegian (NCL), P&O, Royal Caribbean and Thomson Cruises. Although not generally associated with family-style cruising, Cunard also offers children's facilities, including a nanny service, aboard the *QE2*.

On the other hand, if you intend travelling with a child who readily makes their own amusement and enjoys an educational – as opposed to a merely entertaining – experience, don't discount a line that caters primarily to adults. Most companies, even if they do not actively market to children, are not unwelcoming. Indeed, children who are, inadvertently, something of a novelty aboard often acquire a celebrity status.

Information on Family Cruising

For further reading on family holidays afloat, a comprehensive guide called *Cruising with Children* is available from **Travel with Your Children** (45 W. 18th St., 7th Floor Tower, New York, NY 10011, USA. Tel: (+1) 212-206-0688).

Travelling Arrangements for Families

Most cruise lines classify anyone up to and including the age of **16** as a child and will offer varying reductions on their fares, although some only offer child rates for **under-11** year-olds. Many companies do not, however, permit **babies** (although the age classification differs from line to line) and most stipulate that **under-18s** must be accompanied by an adult over the age of 21, although not neccessarily occupying the same cabin. If you are travelling with **someone else's children** (even a child of a partner's previous marriage), be sure to get a letter of permission from the absent parent for the child to board the ship (and/or plane). Your holiday could be stalled at the gangway without it.

Cruising for the Disabled

Although many cruise lines (and airlines) are trying to improve their services for disabled travellers, cruising, by its very nature, poses unique difficulties for those with handicaps. Traditional ships have narrow corridors, steep stairways and awkwardly shaped cabins; fire- and water-tight doors can be heavy and cumbersome to open; exterior decks may be slippery and uneven; and some ship doorways have raised thresholds to combat flooding – obstacles for wheelchairs, walking frames and those with impaired vision.

However, a reasonable percentage of (particularly newer) ships are actually remarkably accessible. Ship design is becoming more open plan, with wider corridors and door frames, more elevators (and even escalators) and fewer raised (or 'lipped') door sills. Major public rooms and lounges are increasingly located on one or two decks only, thus minimizing the need to move up and down between levels. Plus, almost all new ships offer wheelchair accessible cabins and a few also offer special facilities for passengers with hearing difficulties.

Arguably the **best-equipped ships** for disabled passengers of all descriptions are CRYSTAL CRUISE'S *Crystal Harmony* and *Symphony*; P&O's *Oriana*; CUNARD'S *Queen*

USEFUL PUBLICATIONS FOR DISABLED CRUISERS

- *Wheels and Waves: A Cruise-Ferry Guide for the Physically Handicapped* by Genie and George Aroyan, published by **Wheels Aweigh** (17105 San Carlos Boulevard, Suite A-6107, Ft. Myers Beach, FL 33931, USA. tel: (+1) 800-637-2256).
- *Nothing Ventured – Disabled People Travel the World* by **Harrap Columbus** (Chelsea House, 26 Market Square, Bromley, Kent BR1 1NA, England. tel: (+44) 0181-313-3484).
- *Travelin' Talk Directory* – a reference book for the disabled, published by **Travelin' Talk** (Box 3534, Clarksville, TN 37043, USA. tel: (+1) 615-552-6670).
- *Directory of Travel Agencies for the Disabled*, and *Wheelchair Vagabond*, a collection of travel tips, both published by **Twin Peaks Press** (Box 129, Vancouver, WA 98666, Canada. tel: (+1) 206-694-2462).
- The US-based travel companies **Accessible Journeys** and **Flying Wheels Travel** both specialize in booking worldwide cruises for disabled passengers.

> **Tips for Disabled Passengers**
>
> • You will almost certainly need to provide your **own wheelchair**. Some ships insist that this is collapsible and/or narrow gauge.
> • Bring a (collapsible) pointer or other prosthetic device to reach elevator buttons and closet clothes racks.
> • Remember any vital **medications**.
> • Be sure to inform your cruise line and, if applicable, your airline(s), of your disability, together with any special requirements, when you make your reservation. It is also worth **double-checking** this information prior to your departure. Keep **written confirmation** of any promises made about special cabin assignments, airport transfers and so on.

Elizabeth 2 and *Royal Viking Sun*; and PRINCESS CRUISES' *Crown* -, *Dawn* -, *Grand* -, *Regal* - and *Sun Princess*. Good disabled facilities are also found on board CARNIVAL'S *Destiny*; CELEBRITY'S *Constellation*, *Galaxy*, *Horizon* and *Zenith*; COSTA'S *Costa Classica*, *-Romantica* and *-Victoria*; DEUTSCHE SEEREEDEREI'S *Aida*; HAPAG-LLOYD'S *Europa*; HOLLAND AMERICA'S *Maasdam*; NCL'S *Norway* and *Norwegian Crown*; and ROYAL CARIBBEAN'S *Enchantment*-, *Grandeur* -, *Legend* -, *Rhapsody* - and *Splendour of the Seas*.

Hearing- and Vision-Impaired Passengers

Few cruise line brochures mention hearing or sight impairments when referring to passengers with disabilities. The blind, in particular, seem to get the raw deal – there is very rarely any information (including menus) in **braille** and, although some ships permit **guide dogs** on board, quarantine regulations are likely to prevent the dog being allowed ashore in foreign ports (ask about policies on guide dogs before making your reservation).

For those with **hearing** difficulties, the major problem concerns missing announcements made over the public address system and being potentially unaware of an emergency situation. If you are deaf, and even if you are travelling accompanied, do make sure your cabin steward and/or other members of the ship's personnel are aware of your condition, so they know to alert you if ever the alarm bells ring.

NORWEGIAN CRUISE LINE (NCL) is the forerunner in acknowledging the needs of hearing-impaired passengers with 30 special cabins on both the *Norwegian Dream* and *Norwegian Wind*. The *Queen Elizabeth 2* also has special illuminated signs in certain cabins. The *Crystal Harmony*, *Crystal Symphony* and the *Century* each offer hearing-impaired headsets in their cinemas and many ships have electronic display boards for games such as bingo.

Guidelines for Disabled Cruisers

As a disabled cruiser, you will need to be especially discerning in your choice of cruise and ship. The following list outlines some aspects of cruising you will want to check out before you book or when you get aboard. Above all, don't rely on information given to you by your travel agent, especially if the agent does not generally book cruises for people with your particular needs. It is often worthwhile to call the cruise line direct and double-check any detail that is important to you.

- Check that all public rooms and (especially) outside deck/pool areas are **wheelchair accessible**.
- Check the **dimensions** of the doors and especially bathroom doors in your proposed cabin. Frames should be at least 71cm (28in) wide, and ideally over 76cm (30in) wide, to accommodate a standard wheelchair.
- Choose a cabin as close to the **elevators** as possible, or one on the muster station deck or lifeboat embarkation deck, which can offer the peace of mind of not needing to rely on assistance in a general emergency situation.
- If you don't want to miss out on venturing ashore, avoid itineraries that involve '**tender ports**' (that is, when the ship must anchor and the passengers are transported ashore by small tenders or launches).
- Consider an itinerary in **calmer waters** (such as a cruise through Alaska's Inside Passage or a river trip through Europe, up the Amazon or the Mississippi).
- Be sure to inform the maître d' when you make your **table reservation** that you require easy access and wheelchair space.
- Check if the **showroom** seating plan allows good visibility from a wheelchair-allocated space (this could be important if the nightly shows are a highlight for you).
- Many ships require that you travel with an **able-bodied companion** if you use a wheelchair. Be sure to get the okay in advance if you intend travelling alone.

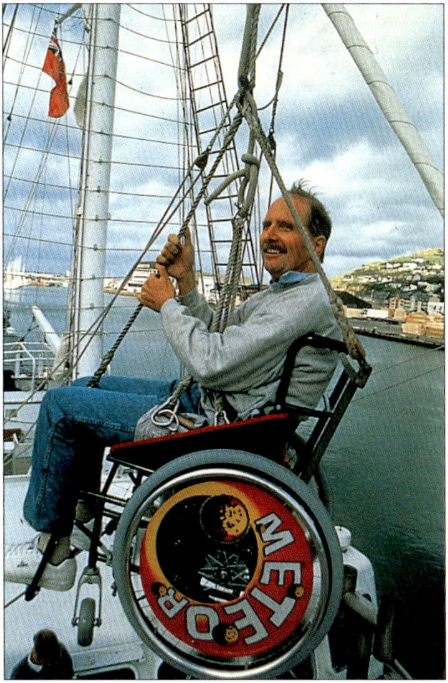

Above: *Scaling the rigging aboard the historic* Lord Nelson.

JUBILEE SAILING TRUST

Although most explorer vessels and sailing ships are not suitable for the handicapped, a notable exception is the JUBILEE SAILING TRUST'S *Lord Nelson* – a beautiful schooner, specially constructed to accommodate approximately 40 disabled (including blind) and able-bodied passengers, who assist the small permanent crew in navigating the waters of the Mediterranean and the Caribbean.

Seniors Discounts

When going ashore to visit a new destination or take part in an organized tour, over-60s may be entitled to certain shoreside **discounts**, such as reduced admission fees or transportation fares. Don't forget that you will need **proof of age** – especially as cruising makes you feel years younger!

Cruising for Seniors

A cruise can provide a marvellous holiday environment for older people, with plenty of entertainment, escorted group shore excursions and a floating hotel that transports you between destinations.

Your **choice of ship** and **itinerary** is all-important, however, and mature passengers wishing to avoid boisterous family-style cruises would do well to opt for a river or coastal vessel or a line such as Cunard, Fred Olsen, Holland America or Crystal Cruises. The cruising division of Saga Holidays, having recently acquired the *Saga Rose*, offers some fascinating itineraries that are strictly for the over-50s, while certain travel companies (such as **SeniorTours**) specialize in cruises for retired people. Some cruise lines supply **gentlemen hosts** as bridge and dance partners – a welcome addition for mature, single ladies (*see* Cruising for Singles).

Older cruisers should also be aware that some lines, such as Royal Caribbean, offer **special discounted rates** for seniors, as do US-based membership organizations such as the American Association of Retired Persons or the National Council of Senior Citizens. Cruising discounts for seniors are also listed in the monthly newsletter, *The Mature Traveler* (PO Box 50820, Reno, NV 89513, USA. Tel: (+1) 702-786-7419).

Below: *Showing some mean skills at the original deck game, shuffleboard.*

Making the Most of Your Cruise

As well as making sure you find suitable accommodation aboard (see Box), there are a few other aspects of cruising of particular relevance to seniors. Those with **medical conditions** should be aware that, despite the fact that some ships have excellent medical facilities, cruises are unsuitable for those who are bed-ridden or have a serious, recurring medical complaint. Vessels without an official doctor (such as cargo ships) may also impose upper age limits. In addition, specific types of medications may not be available on board – be sure to take enough of any prescribed drugs, together with more mundane but crucial items such as an extra hearing-aid battery, spare pair of glasses and spare dentures

On a cruise it is all too easy to over-eat, over-drink, over-exercise and generally **over-indulge**. Be sensible and know your capabilities. Ask the shore excursion manager to recommend tours that are not too strenuous; take it easy on the dance floor and don't make drastic changes to your regular eating, drinking and sleeping pattern.

Above: *P&O's* Oriana, *well-known for its classical music theme cruises.*

Themed Cruises

For passengers with special hobbies or interests, there are many ships on the market offering a wide choice of theme or specialist cruises. This can be a wonderful way of combining your particular area of interest with a holiday at sea. It can also be the perfect means of meeting people with whom you share a common link – for singles, in particular, theme cruises provide a very integrated environment in the company of like-minded individuals. Lectures or performances by leading guest specialists and the opportunity to meet these experts in a social setting are always a highlight of this type of cruise.

Music

The **classical music** cruises aboard Costa's *Mermoz* (*see* Box) and P&O's *Oriana* are probably the best known and most popular form of musical cruises. The latter, hosted by British television presenter **Richard Baker**, features live concerts and related lectures. In a similar vein, Noble Caledonia's musical river cruises through Europe are presented by broadcaster **John Amis**, and include appropriate excursions and (often operatic) onboard performances. Host of the **Van Cliburn Piano**

Music on *Mermoz*

Arguably the most exciting classical music cruise is the one held every year aboard the lovely *Mermoz*. Recently acquired by Costa from Croisieres Paquet, not only does this vessel offer shore excursions to selected concerts in inspirational locations, she also features on-board talks and performances by some of the world's most celebrated musicians. **Isaac Stern**, **Mystislav Rostropovich**, **Maurice André** and **Vladimir Ashkenazy** have all trodden the decks of this cultural *grande dame*.

Competition, SEABOURN CRUISES frequently offers classical music entertainment, as does SWAN HELLENIC, CUNARD and HAPAG-LLOYD. These are also good bets for **opera** buffs.

NCL's *Norway* features **Big Band**, **Rock and Roll** and **Country and Western** cruises in an impressive programme of musical themes that includes an annual **Floating Jazz Festival** – arguably the best of its kind and featuring many contemporary jazz giants; PREMIER and COMMODORE CRUISE LINES both host specialist music cruises including **Country**, **Blues**, **Big Band**, **Motown** and **Jazz**; SEABOURN and CUNARD also offer jazz cruises and the DELTA QUEEN STEAMBOAT COMPANY is known for its regular **Dixie** and **Big Band** river cruises.

BOOKING A THEME CRUISE

- Theme cruises tend to be **irregularly scheduled**, so don't depend on a certain cruise following the same itinerary from one month or one year to the next.
- Get confirmed **details** of themed cruises from the cruise line in question – don't just go by the brochures as there could be late changes.
- A good place to find out information about themed cruises is in **specialist magazines** of your particular interest or hobby.

Sports and Fitness

NORWEGIAN CRUISE LINE (NCL) leads the way when it comes to sports themes. When not catering to music-lovers, the *Norway* runs an impressive selection of sporting cruises, including **football**, **tennis**, **hockey**, **basketball**, **baseball**, **volleyball** – and even **skiing** and **motor-racing**. NCL's *Norwegian Dream* also provides specialist holidays for golfers, as do the fleets of ROYAL CARIBBEAN and CLIPPER CRUISES.

The DELTA QUEEN STEAMBOAT COMPANY operates **baseball**-themed cruises in the summer and **Kentucky Derby** specials in the spring. Its traditional paddle-wheel steamers are even something of a theme in themselves and even participate in their own sporting event – the annual **Great Steamboat Race** on the Mississippi River.

Nature and the Environment

Many coastal and expedition ships offer worldwide destinations of specific interest to environmentalists and nature-lovers and even mainstream cruise lines feature nature-related programmes. ORIENT LINES and AMERICAN HAWAII CRUISES, for example, offer penguin-spotting and whale-watching trips respectively.

Above: *Cruise passengers taking the chance to get a little closer to nature.*
Opposite: *Dixie-style river cruising on the Mississippi.*

These types of holidays are frequently advertised in relevant **specialist magazines**, such as those of nature/wildlife organizations. In the UK, details of bird-watching cruises (offered by companies such as SWAN HELLENIC and NOBLE CALEDONIA) can be found among the pages of the **RSPB**'s magazine, *Birds*, and conservation-themed cruises in conjunction with PAGE & MOY are advertised in *The National Trust Magazine*.

Other Themes

ABERCROMBIE & KENT, SEABOURN, FRED OLSEN, SWAN HELLENIC and charterers such as CLASSICAL CRUISES and VOYAGES OF DISCOVERY offer holidays specialising in **Art**, **Architecture** or **Archeology**; HOLLAND AMERICA LINE operates several **photography**-themed cruises; COMMODORE hosts **Cajun**-theme, '**Oktoberfest**', **Square Dance** cruises and even a **Twins Cruise** for twins and triplets; CUNARD, SWAN HELLENIC and CELEBRITY provide cruises for **food and wine** buffs; FRED OLSEN offers **indoor games** themes; BERJAYA schedules **beauty pageants** amongst its theme cruises; SEABOURN schedules **current affairs** and **political** cruises; CELEBRITY even provides **virtual-reality** cabins on its hi-tech 'Cyber' Cruises; and for just about any theme (from **personal finance** to **murder mystery**) look out for the ever-fascinating programme of CUNARD's *Queen Elizabeth 2*.

RMS St Helena

Boasting the almost-forgotten sobriquet 'Royal Mail Ship', CURNOW SHIPPING's *RMS St Helena* is a 100-passenger cargo vessel which sails between Cardiff and Cape Town, with stops at Tenerife and the rarely visited South Atlantic islands of St Helena, Ascension Island and Tristan da Cunha. As the final home of Napoleon, St Helena has particular interest for **historians**, while St Helena and Tristan da Cunha are unusual stops for keen **naturalists**. For both these remote islands, which have no air strip, the ship is the only regular supply link for goods and passengers.

CUNARD
Queen Elizabeth 2

5
The Cruise Lines

The cruise industry is comprised of numerous lines and operators, offering widely differing holidays to far-flung destinations by way of diverse itineraries and boats both large and small, old and new. However, some of the main players in this diverse market share important common features: CARNIVAL CRUISE LINES, CELEBRITY CRUISES, HOLLAND AMERICA LINE, PRINCESS CRUISES and ROYAL CARIBBEAN INTERNATIONAL, for example, are all US-based, US-marketed companies, offering mainstream, affordable cruises aboard new, high passenger-carry ships. These, together with CUNARD LINE, COSTA CRUISES, NORWEGIAN CRUISE LINE, P&O CRUISES, STAR CRUISE and CRYSTAL CRUISES are the current fore-runners in an ever-changing industry.

This chapter provides a brief introduction to these leading players, as well as other major – and minor – cruise lines of the world. Addresses, telephone numbers and web sites for the lines listed here can be found in pages 170–4. Information on companies offering cruises in cargo and sailing ships, riverboats and explorer vessels pages can be found in Chapter 8.

African Safari Club

The petite and charming 200-passenger *Royal Star* offers year-round cruising in the Indian Ocean. Operated by the large hotel and tourism group, African Safari Club, she sails out of Mombasa on a series of itineraries to the Seychelles, Mascarenes, Comores, Madagascar, the Maldives, Sri Lanka and India. Launched in 1956, *Royal*

CRUISING AGENTS

The list of the industry's travel agents, sales agents and charterers is inexhaustible, but the following companies are among those who have become synonymous with cruise travel:

- **Classical Cruises** markets special interest cruises with an educational theme in the USA and charters ships such as SWAN HELLENIC's *Minerva*.
- **Equity Cruises** is the UK sales agent for CARNIVAL CRUISE LINES, HOLLAND AMERICA LINE and METRO HOLDINGS.
- **Esplanade Tours** is the north American sales agent for SPICE ISLAND CRUISES and NOBLE CALEDONIA.
- **Eurocruises** specializes in marketing the fleets of European operators in North America. These include FRED OLSEN, KRISTINA CRUISES, GRIMALDI CRUISES, FESTIVAL CRUISES and ARCALIA SHIPPING.

(continued on page 73)

Opposite: *The unmistakeable livery of CUNARD's flagship, the* QE2.

Above: *AIRTOURS CRUISE's* Sundream, *a 23,000grt ship built in 1970.*

Star provides a casual, comfortable cruise in traditional surroundings which can be combined with pre- and post-cruise land and safari packages.

Airtours Cruises

Airtours bought its first ship – NCL's *Southward* – in 1994. Re-named *Seawing*, the 900 plus-passenger ship was put into service in the Mediterranean, where she was joined by the larger, sleeker *Carousel* (formerly *Nordic Prince*) and her sister ship, *Sundream* (formerly *Song of Norway*), combining Mediterranean cruises out of Mallorca and winter itineraries in the Caribbean.

Airtours has set out to make cruising accessible to British families, young couples and first-time passengers by making value for money its first priority. The company has the advantage of operating its own transportation network, including aeroplanes and transfer buses, and as a well-established tour operator it promotes cruise-and-stay packages with a week on the ship and a week in a hotel. Airtours does not claim to offer a sophisticated travel experience – this is cruising with a boisterous ambience, casual dress code and entertainment provided by the hard-working social staff, who also run a range of children's programmes divided according to age-group.

THE AIRTOURS NETWORK

The multi-layered ownership of sections of the cruise industry can be seen in the role played by AIRTOURS. A sizeable stake in this rapidly developing company is owned by the massive CARNIVAL CORPORATION, while AIRTOURS itself – already the parent of travel operations like Going Places in the UK, Scandinavia's AB Leisure Group and Canada's Sunquest Vacations – has joined CARNIVAL in buying COSTA CRUISES and now aims to become the biggest package tour operator in North America.

American Hawaii Cruises

This all-American cruise line offers possibly the most romantic way to island-hop around Hawaii, with year-round cruises out of Honolulu. Currently owned by the Delta Queen Steamboat Company (and jointly trading as American Classic Voyages), American Hawaii operates the *Independence* – an 800-passenger US-registered ship, first launched in 1951 and decorated in authentic regional style, including orchids and tropical plants, a Hawaiian museum, Hawaiian-music jukebox, exhibitions by local artists and instruction by a Kumu (teacher) in local folklore, crafts, dancing the hula and playing the ukulele. The vessel attracts an easy mix of young families, retirees and honeymooners (special wedding packages are offered).

Arcalia Shipping

This Portuguese company operates the cozy *Funchal* – a vessel launched in 1961 which tours the Norwegian fjords, Spitsbergen and the North Cape. With a fine lecture programme, this ship borders on expedition cruising, while still offering a traditional cruise in old-fashioned surroundings for approximately 450 passengers. Having recently taken over the mid-sized *Princess Danae*, Arcalia is also including Caribbean, Mediterranean and South American itineraries in its programmes. Marketed to a destination-orientated, international clientele, both vessels are a good choice for undemanding cruisers content to be on older ships and keen to discover some unusual destinations.

Awani Cruises

A recently formed Indonesian-based cruise line, Awani has taken the former *World Renaissance* and transformed it into *Awani Dream* – 'The Fun Ship'. Sailing out of Jakarta, and catering particularly to the burgeoning domestic market, *Awani Dream* offers mini cruises around the Java Sea. On-board facilities are basic by mainstream standards, but with the emphasis firmly on family fun, watersports and shoreside golf options, the priority is on an action-packed budget break. *Awani Dream* has been joined by a new sister – the former *Cunard Countess*, re-named *Awani Dream II*.

Berjaya Holiday Cruise

This Kuala Lumpur-based line operates the petite *Coral Princess* on a series of short cruises to Phuket, Penang, Hat Yai, Singapore, Langkawi and Port Klang. Berjaya

CRUISING AGENTS

(continued from page 71)

- **Festive Cruises** (not to be confused with FESTIVAL CRUISES) regularly charters Arcalia Shipping's *Funchal* for a series of itineraries in northern Europe, with sailings out of the UK.
- **Golden Bear Travel** is the north American sales agent for HAPAG-LLOYD.
- **Neckermann Seereisen** is the German charterer of vessels such as CARAVELLA SHIPPING'S *Astra II*.
- **OdessAmerica** is the US sales agent for GALAPAGOS CRUISE LINE and CRUCEROS ASTRALIS.
- **Page & Moy** markets predominantly European and special interest cruises in the UK and charters ships such as the Greek-owned *Ocean Majesty* – a lively, sometimes crowded, vessel providing traditional mid-scale cruising.
- **Seetours International** is a German charterer and cruise marketing agent.
- **Voyages Jules Verne** markets in the UK various riverboats and the ships of LEISURE CRUISES and AFRICAN SAFARI CLUB.

Addresses and contact numbers for all these agents are found under 'Useful Addresses' on pages 170–4.

> **TALL TALES**
>
> Unless you specifically request it – and in spite of cruising's romantic image – don't expect to find a double bed in your cabin. Beds are usually single and rather small and even suites may only boast a queen-size. If you are very tall, very big or very amorous, check the sleeping arrangements before you book. Requests can usually be accommodated (and beds often zipped together), but don't wait until you get on the ship. Families with young children should opt for a cabin with additional fold-away bunks (put the kids on top and they'll love climbing up the ladder!). These are not such a good option for adults, however, unless they are young, agile and don't intend spending much time in the cabin.

is well-known in the domestic market for its excellent theme cruises, and *Coral Princess* is also the official cruise liner for various major international beauty pageants. The ship, launched in 1962 but rebuilt in 1991, boasts a lively ambience and a range of leisure facilities including a VIP gaming room, sports centre, karaoke lounge and children's amenities. Berjaya is also the parent company of Kuala Lumpur-based Empress Cruise Lines.

Black Sea Shipping Company (BLASCO)

This Odessa-based company operates a large fleet of mainly mid-sized ships of middle age or older, including *Dimitriy Shostakovich*, *Shota Rustaveli*, *Kareliya* and *Azerbaydzhan*. While these vessels offer interesting European itineraries and a convivial ambience, they are unsuited to those seeking a sophisticated, up-market experience. Cruisers on a budget and those preferring an informal atmosphere should, however, enjoy the genuine Ukrainian hospitality.

Canaveral Cruise Line

When the Kosmas Shipping Corporation purchased the mid-sized vintage *Dolphin IV* (launched in 1956) from Dolphin Cruise Line in 1995, it named its new line Canaveral after its new base port in Florida, USA. The resulting cruises between Port Canaveral and the Bahamas are of the lively and crowded 'mini' variety and incorporate pre- and post-cruise options in Florida.

> **CARNIVAL CAROUSING**
>
> Night owls never go hungry aboard CARNIVAL's mega-ships: after the midnight buffet they can grab a bite at the 01:30 buffet! Stamina can also have its rewards for gamblers aboard CARNIVAL's *Ecstasy*, which has over 200 slot machines.

Caravella Shipping

Catering to a predominantly Russian and German-speaking clientele, Caravella operates competitively priced cruises in Mediterranean waters aboard the *Astra*. Launched in 1965, she provides a casual, port-intensive cruise experience for up to 282 passengers. Her larger, younger and more sophisticated sister, *Astra II* (formerly *Golden Odyssey*) is frequently under charter to Neckermann Seereisen, offering a series of cruises around the Mediterranean and Baltic.

Carnival Cruise Lines

The largest and (according to its own publicity) 'most popular cruise line in the world', Carnival is the proverbial all-American success story – a company that grew from one ageing vessel into a multi-billion-dollar fleet, carrying over 25 per cent of all cruise ship passengers. The mark of Carnival are mega-ships such as the 2000-plus passenger *Fantasy*, *Ecstasy*, *Sensation*, *Fascination*, *Imagination* and *Inspiration*, not to mention the huge *Carnival Triumph*, presently the largest cruise ship in the world, and *Carnival Destiny*, a former holder of the title. Every public space is flamboyantly and thematically decorated, with wide promenades and towering atriums featuring huge, kinetic sculptures something of a Carnival trademark. If you like Las Vegas, you will love Carnival.

THE CARNIVAL AIN'T OVER

The rags-to-riches story of CARNIVAL began in 1972, when the line's founder, Ted Arison, joined forces with a Boston travel company to buy a 900-passenger ship, the *Empress of Canada*. Renamed *Mardi Gras*, she was to embody Arison's ideal of unstuffy, high-energy, affordable vacations for people who had never before dreamed of taking a cruise. Within 10 years Arison had ordered the first of the brand new 'fun ships', the 1000-passenger *Tropicale*. Then came the *Carnival Destiny* – the 101,000grt vessel with the claim to fame of being the world's largest cruise ship (until the launch of the *Grand Princess*) and the first to be too big to transit the Panama Canal. Her successors, *Elation* and *Paradise* were a 'mere' 70,000grt apiece, but the launch of the gargantuan *Carnival Triumph* marks the return of the 'world's biggest' title to Carnival.

Left: *The dazzling Las Vegas-style atrium on board* Carnival Destiny.

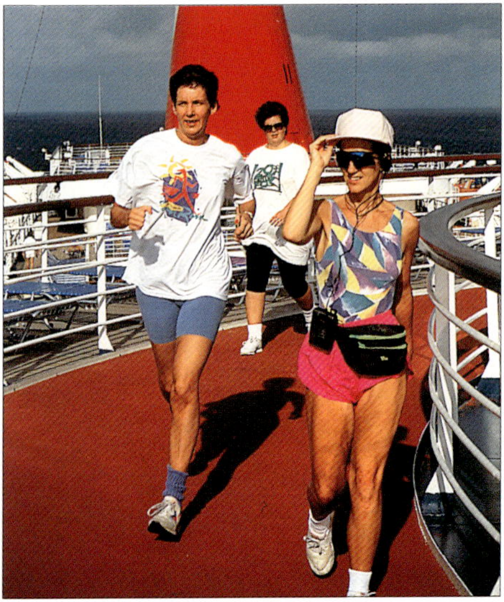

Above: *The innovative exercise track on* Carnival Sensation *– popular with joggers and walkers alike.*

Unsurprisingly, given the Vegas parallel, the casino occupies a huge amount of space on these ships – as does the shopping mall, complete with boutiques and jewellery stores. Excellent fitness facilities include innovative banked and padded jogging tracks and huge spas, offering hi-tech, supervised gymnasium equipment and the latest treatments. Plus, unlike the 'dip pools' of other lines, Carnival swimming pools are actually big enough to swim in and even feature water slides.

Children are well catered for in these floating theme parks and 'Camp Carnival' offers a year-round programme of supervised activities, classified according to age group. Even teenagers will enjoy the lively ambience, along with their own discos and impressive video arcades that feature some of cruising's first virtual reality machines. As for the grown-ups, non-stop activities abound and night-time entertainment is impressive, with large-production shows, dancing and varied live music options.

Although Carnival attracts a wide cross-section of passengers, these are casual, glitzy cruises aimed at sun-seeking party-animals rather than culture or wildlife buffs and they attract a high proportion of first-time cruisers and singles. Hardly surprising then that the company has its feet firmly in Caribbean waters, including the Mexican Riviera and Bahamas, with a toe-hold in Alaska, Hawaii and the Panama Canal.

'X' MARKS THE SPOT

Each CELEBRITY ship boasts a distinctive white 'X' on its stack – the reason for this is that X is the Greek equivalent of the letter 'C', the initial of both Celebrity and its Greek parent company, Chandris.

Celebrity Cruises

Celebrity is the relatively recent creation of the long-established Greek parent company, the Chandris Group, and has recently been acquired by RCI. The line has firmly established itself as a leader in cruising's vast middle market, with itineraries revolving mainly around the Caribbean, but also including Alaska, the Panama Canal and round trips between New York and Bermuda.

In many ways, the line's development parallels that of the whole cruise industry – from the comfortable, mid-sized *Meridian* (launched in 1963 and recently sold to Metro Holdings of Singapore) to the larger, well-appointed *Horizon* and *Zenith* (launched 1990 and 1992 respectively), to the latest 70,000+grt *Century*, *Galaxy* and *Mercury*. The latter vessels boast hi-tech electronic facilities, resulting from a venture with the Sony Corporation of America, that justify their claim as 'ships for the 21st century'. Conference amenities, state-of-the-art spas, touch-screen information booths, customized 'video wallpaper', interactive cabin television service and futuristic entertainment facilities are integral features of Celebrity's latest fleet additions.

In keeping with its lengthy pedigree, however, Celebrity still offers what is basically a traditional cruise experience. Evenings are elegant, decor is stylish, gentleman hosts partner single ladies on the dance floor and on-board activities and entertainments include something for families with children, young and middle-aged couples, singles and seniors.

WHIZZ! BANG! CRASH!

An increasingly standard feature on mega-ships are hi-tech video arcades. Virtual reality machines, video games and sports simulators are a big hit with many younger passengers, particularly on well-equipped vessels such as CARNIVAL'S *Holiday* or CELEBRITY'S *Century* and *Galaxy*. CELEBRITY'S exclusive contract with America's Sony Corporation means that their ships boast all kinds of electronic gadgetry, including the latest in virtual reality.

Commodore Cruise Line

Having come through various recent changes and mergers, Commodore now offers some consistency with weekly sailings out of New Orleans. The *Enchanted Isle* offers year-round cruising in the western Caribbean, with pre- and post-cruise options in New Orleans. Built in 1958 and accommodating approximately 800 passengers, *Enchanted Isle* offers an intimate on-board atmosphere and some

Below: *A hat to remember for some COMMODORE passengers ashore on Cozumel Island, off Mexico's Caribbean coast.*

When With the Romans . . .

Aboard a Costa ship, you will be left in little doubt as to its national allegiances. The ambience is lively, the decor hints at the Renaissance and special touches include changeable restaurant 'scenery' and Venetian Carnival Night or Roman Bacchanal evenings (with the majority of passengers sporting togas).

of the most affordable deals on the market. She has recently been joined by the former Regency Cruises' ship, *Regent Sun* – a slightly newer vessel of similar size and style. Families are well-catered for in a casual, fun-in-the-sun style of cruising and, with its inclusive wedding packages, occasional singles' cruises and themed events ranging from Square Dancing to Oktoberfests, Big Band to Country or Blues, Commodore also attracts a wide cross-section of passengers who might otherwise never have even considered setting foot on a ship.

Below: Costa Riviera *alongside in the popular cruise destination of the US Virgin Islands.*

Costa Cruises

The large American-based Costa Cruises is an expansion of parent company, **Costa Crociere** – a long-established Italian cruise line. Costa's fleet can be subdivided into four pairs of 'sisters': the traditional, mid-sized *Costa Playa* and *Costa Riviera*; the mid-sized *Costa Marina* and *Costa Allegra*; the large *Costa Classica* and *Costa Romantica*; and the extra-large *Costa Victoria* and *Costa Olympia*. With the exception of the comfortably ageing *Costa Playa* and *Costa Riviera*, all these vessels have launch dates after 1990, making this one of the newest fleets in the world. Costa have also recently acquired the ageing, though characterful, *Mermoz*, famed for her classical music theme cruises.

The fleet's itineraries feature the Caribbean, the Mediterranean, the Baltic, South America and transatlantic cruises. Traditionalists may decry the angular lines of Costa's more recent additions (particularly the *Marina* and *Allegra*), but the line offers up-beat facilities, a varied entertainment programme and good Italian-style dining for a fair price.

Cruise Lines International

Competing in the burgeoning eastern marketplace, CLI operates short, year-round cruises around Southeast Asia aboard the modern, mid-sized *Nautican* (formerly *Crown Monarch*). This vessel provides a comfortable, informal cruise experience in attractive surroundings for those seeking a reasonably priced break in an exotic setting.

Above: *The bright and elegant Palm Court lounge on* Crystal Harmony.

Crystal Cruises

American-based Crystal was formed in 1988 by the Japanese NYK (Nippon Yusen Kaisha) company, one of the oldest and largest shipping lines in the world. *Crystal Harmony* was launched in 1990 and her sister ship, *Crystal Symphony*, five years later. Both vessels are large (around 50,000grt and carrying up to 1000 passengers apiece) and luxuriously appointed. Excellent service, fine dining, dazzling entertainment and discreet pampering have become as much Crystal hallmarks as the turquoise seahorses that grace each stack.

Catering predominantly to a mature, sophisticated international clientele who expect – and are prepared to pay for – a quality experience, the ships have spacious, elegant lounges, business facilities and Italian and Asian restaurants. Evening entertainment intersperses first-rate production shows with classical concerts and big band music, while daytime activities include Crystal Visions Enrichment Lecture Series and Crystal University at Sea (featuring renowned speakers on a diversity of subjects). Crystal itineraries are equally diverse, including South and Central America and the Panama Canal, the Mediterranean, northern Europe, Alaska, the US east coast, Hawaii and an annual world cruise.

Spa Specials

The *Crystal Harmony*, *Crystal Symphony*, *Queen Elizabeth 2* and the newest Royal Caribbean and Costa ships all house fine examples of shipboard spas. Most spas or health and beauty centres, however, are not operated 'in house' but, rather by a concessionaire such as Steiners, Golden Door or Champneys. Of these companies, Steiners – which recently incorporated Coiffeur Transocean – has impressive facilities aboard the *Century* and *Galaxy*, the *Norway* and throughout the Carnival fleet. Note that hairdressing and beauty treatments are **not included** in the cost of your cruise – a list of charges should be available at the salon or spa reception desk.

THE QE2

As one might expect, 'the Queen' offers a wealth of idiosyncratic amenities, including a florist, computer centre, synagogue, garage (with space for 16 cars), branch of *Harrods* and kennels – complete with dogs' lamp-post! She also boasts a unique Heritage Trail (displaying memorabilia of former Cunarders) and possibly the best-equipped hospital and library at sea. *QE2's* facilities are accessible to all passengers, although the allocation of the five restaurants (all single sitting) is determined by cabin grade.

Cunard Line

It is impossible to mention Cunard without reference to its famous pedigree. Founded by Samuel Cunard in 1840, this fleet ruled the waves during the golden age of the great liners, carrying a continuous succession of rich, celebrated and royal passengers on year-round transatlantic crossings and global navigations.

Approximately 200 vessels have sailed under the Cunard flag, many of them stars in their own right – although in today's cruising world, Cunard is one of the few major lines with a diminishing fleet. Following recent upheavals, the sale of several ships and its subsequent take-over by the giant Carnival Corporation, the line has been streamlined and is now concentrating firmly on the upper echelons of the market. In terms of shapes and sizes, however, the fleet is still diverse and the corporate move to Florida from its New York base implies a further – and literal – change of direction.

Cunard's flagship is the inimitable *Queen Elizabeth 2*. The last of the great liners and still the most famous ship in the world, this *grand dame* is guaranteed star billing at every port of call and is the only ship to offer a regular service across the Atlantic Ocean by the traditional northern route. In contrast to this mighty flagship, the diminutive *Sea Goddess I* and *Sea Goddess II* epitomise the 'private yacht' ambience of a very small

Right: *CUNARD's well-appointed mid-sized ship* Vistafjord.

vessel, with the mid-sized *Royal Viking Sun* and *Vistafjord* completing the fleet.

Unrestricted to specific regions, the Cunard fleet offers worldwide itineraries, including annual circumnavigations by the *QE2* and the *Royal Viking Sun*. While not for budget travellers, young families or those seeking a casual style of vacation, these cruises are ideal for those who prefer – and can afford – a traditional, elegant, service-based, five-star holiday experience.

Above: *CUNARD's luxurious small yacht-like* Sea Goddess I, *lit up by the quayside.*

Deilmann Reederei

The company founded in 1968 by Peter Deilmann offers one of the industry's most diverse fleets – a series of deluxe European riverboats, a beautiful three-masted barquentine (*Lili Marleen*) and two cruise ships.

The first of these cruise ships, *Berlin*, is the star of Germany's long-running television series, *Traumschiff* ('Dream Ship' – the German equivalent of *The Love Boat*). A diminutive 420-passenger vessel, she provides an upscale, elegant cruise experience for a predominantly German-speaking clientele. Her new sister is the *Deutschland* – a larger, 650-passenger ship, offering equally diverse worldwide itineraries. For a ship launched in 1998, *Deutschland* promises a surprisingly nostalgic 1920s ambience.

COMMONLY ASKED CRUISING QUESTIONS (6)

Q: *Will I be able to attend a religious service?*
A: On longer sailings, and especially during important religious festivals, an interdenominational service may be scheduled and conducted by the Captain or other officiate. Ministers, rabbis or priests travelling as passengers will also occasionally volunteer to conduct a service. Several ships house a small chapel – the QE2 has its own synagogue – and it is often possible to attend services at local places of worship when you are in port.

Taking Children Ashore

Children are expected to be in the care of their parents or guardians when off the ship (if you intend taking the line's organized shore excursions, special junior rates sometimes, but not always, apply). When travelling with children, it is preferable to opt for 'activity' excursions (such as snorkelling and boat trips) rather than lengthy bus rides. Full-day coach tours can be too much for very young travellers.

Delphin Seereisen

Providing a comfortably elegant cruise experience for a predominantly German-speaking clientele, *Delphin* (formerly *Kazakhstan II*), offers various itineraries in the Mediterranean, northern Europe and Caribbean, as well as a magnificent 150-day world cruise. Launched in 1975, this attractive, mid-sized vessel is ideally suited to those seeking port-intensive cruises at a realistic price.

Deutsche Seereederei

An East German government company before the reunification, Deutsche Seereederei is now part of a large German conglomerate of travel and tourism companies and operator of the *Arkona* and *Aida*. The *Arkona* is a mid-sized ship launched in 1981 which is frequently under charter to German operators. Offering a very traditional cruise experience, she boasts fine facilities and port-intensive global itineraries that should appeal to the serious sightseer. Attractive as she is, however, it is her younger sister – the 1996-launched *Aida* – that is the focus of most attention.

The only cruise ship with a face painted on her hull, *Aida* offers a 'resort club' style of cruise, attracting vast numbers of youthful, active German-speaking singles, couples and young families. Some 90 per cent of *Aida's* passengers are experienced travellers but first-time cruis-

Right: *The unmistakeable face of* DEUTSCHE SEEREEDEREI*'s exciting new flagship* Aida.

ers, tempted by the promise of unstuffy, unstructured holiday fun. Casual but not budget, with the emphasis on buffet dining and adventure-orientated excursions, this 1200-passenger ship spends her summers in the Mediterranean (out of Palma de Mallorca) and winters in the Caribbean (out of the Dominican Republic).

Dining with Disney

The restaurants aboard *Disney Magic* include elegant French-style 'Lumière's', casual Caribbean-style 'Parrot Cay', 'Palo', an adults-only Italian restaurant, and the amazing California-themed 'Animator's Palate', where the entire room changes from black and white to glorious technicolour during the course of your meal! One of the innovations aboard the ship is that passengers dine at a different restaurant every night of their cruise.

Disney Cruise Line

With the 1998 launch of *Disney Magic*, this famous company is now making a splash in the world of family cruising – and with a ship that cuts a surprisingly nostalgic figure. Although a hefty 85,000grt, *Disney Magic* boasts elegant lines and two distinctive funnels (one an effective fake!), evocative of the age of the great liners. Inside, the clever blending of high technology and classic decor, together with segregated and integrated adult and junior options, is Disney at its very best.

Distinctive features include spacious accommodations; a grand 1040-seat theatre; full-screen cinema; an interactive sports club with multiple-screen broadcasts; adult-orientated Beat Street, with different styles of live music and off-beat comedy; three pools (including one adults-only); nearly an entire deck of children's facilities and space for age-specific activities; teenagers' coffee bar; and some original dining options (*see* Box).

Sailing out of Port Canaveral, *Disney Magic* visits Nassau and the line's private Bahamian island, Castaway Cay, combining 3- or 4-night cruises with a stay at a Disney resort. A sister ship, *Disney Wonder*, is due to be launched soon.

Empress Cruise Lines

Founded in 1993 under the corporate umbrella of Berjaya Holiday Cruise, this Malaysian line operates the 380-passenger ship, *The Empress* (formerly *Sunward*). Though not for seekers of cruise sophistication, the ship is a comfortable one which offers a series of lively party cruises out of Thailand. Catering primarily to the Malaysian market, the line also attracts passengers from Thailand, Taiwan, Hong Kong and Australia.

Shipboard Photographs

One of the more interesting window displays aboard the ship is likely to belong to the photo shop – where the results of the official photographers' labours are exhibited. Larger vessels will boast a whole team of professionals ready to snap your every move – embarking, disembarking, shaking the captain's hand, posing with costumed entertainers, relaxing on the deck or performing in the lip-sync show. Their photos – including large formal-night portraits – make attractive souvenirs, but they are not cheap. The photo shop may also sell film and camera supplies and offer a speedy film processing service.

Fantasy Cruises

Owned by the Chandris Group (also a parent company of Celebrity Cruises), Fantasy provides competitively priced, easy-going cruising for a mainly European clientele aboard the 20,000grt *Amerikanis*, launched in 1952 as the *Kenya Castle*. A characterful elderly ship with a convivial atmosphere, she offers varied, port-intensive itineraries throughout the Mediterranean and northern Europe and a surprisingly high crew-passenger ratio.

Festival Cruises

Launched in 1993 specifically to target the European market, Greece-based Festival Cruises (marketed in the USA as Azur-Bolero Cruises) offers year-round itineraries throughout the Mediterranean (including the Canary Islands and transits of the Suez and Corinth canals), northern Europe and the Caribbean.

The Festival fleet comprises the 900-passenger *Bolero* (formerly NCL's *Starward*), 780-passenger *The Azur* and 720-passenger *Flamenco* (formerly CTC's *Southern Cross*). A middle-aged trio with original launch dates of 1968, 1971 and 1972 respectively, these comfortable ships provide a traditional cruise experience in convivial, sometimes crowded, surroundings. Good sports facilities, port-intensive itineraries and competitive prices are all features that make Festival particularly suited to active couples, families and first-time cruisers on a budget.

Fred Olsen Cruise Lines

In the mid-1800s, the three Olsen brothers from Norway developed an impressive fleet of sailing ships out of their home port of Hvitsen. With the family name established, the son of one of these brothers, Thomas Fredrik Olsen, was to continue the tradition by founding the line which still bears his name.

Traditional cruising is very much a Fred Olsen hallmark, and in spite of their years, the line's comfortable mid-sized ships *Black Prince* and *Black Watch* attract a faithful following of mainly mature British cruisers. Sailing out of Dover, these ships offer a surprisingly

Above: Black Prince *docked alongside at Funchal in Madeira.*

diverse range of itineraries, including coastal Africa and the Indian Ocean, the Mediterranean and Atlantic islands, northern Europe and the Baltic, the Caribbean, US east coast, South America (including the Amazon), India and Southeast Asia (Vietnam, Indonesia and the Philippines). Regular themed cruises are scheduled in these itineraries and include subjects such as horticulture, classical music and indoor games.

Dining and entertainment are not as sophisticated as on some other vessels, but the ships have been tastefully refurbished and boast distinctive features. *Black Prince*, for example, houses an indoor (as well as an outdoor) swimming pool and an extendable rear marina with water-skiing, windsurfing and sailing facilities.

Golden Sun Cruises

The result of the 1998 amalgamation of the Greek lines Dolphin Hellas and Attika, Golden Sun operates the 670-passenger *Aegean Dolphin* and the 350-passenger *Arcadia*. Sailing predominantly in the Mediterranean but expected to expand into northern Europe and the Caribbean, this fleet promises a basic, lively, mixed European (and therefore, multi-lingual) cruise experience.

Safety First

If safety considerations come high on your list when choosing a cruise, you will find that newer cruise ships tend to be more up to date with safety regulations set by the **International Maritime Organisation** (IMO) than older vessels. By the beginning of the 21st century, for example, all passenger ships must incorporate an anti-fire sprinkler system. New vessels are fitted with sprinklers at the time of construction, but for older ships, complying with this regulation is a costly, and sometimes unviable, prospect. Lifeboats, liferafts and other emergency facilities are also likely to be superior on modern vessels.

A Brief History of Hapag-Lloyd

With a heritage dating back to 1848, the German lines Hapag and Norddeutscher Lloyd between them operated several winners of the prestigious Blue Riband and one of the world's very first passenger cruise ships, Hapag's steamer, *Augusta Victoria*, launched in 1891. The fleet's present flagship, *Europa*, was launched in 1982 and is the fifth ship in the company's history to bear the name.

Grimaldi Cruises

This Italian line offers a variety of Mediterranean itineraries aboard the vintage, mid-sized *Ausonia* – a comfortable ship with plenty of deck space for her sun-loving international passengers. Gamblers may be disappointed by the lack of a casino, but romantic couples, young families, youthful singles and active young-at-heart seniors without overly high expectations will all enjoy these informal, up-beat cruises.

Hapag-Lloyd Cruises

Hapag-Lloyd is the result of the 1970 merger between two distinguished German lines, Hapag and Norddeutscher Lloyd. Their fleet is led by the upscale *Europa*, which offers five-star food and service, single sitting dining, an excellent spa and three swimming pools for up to 600 passengers. *Europa* has been joined by the sleek, 420-passenger *Columbus*, an attractive modern vessel with cruises scheduled on the St Lawrence Seaway and the Great Lakes. In addition, the deluxe explorer vessels, *Hanseatic* and *Bremen*, offer wonderfully off-beat global itineraries to South America, the Arctic and Antarctic. *Hanseatic*, in particular, is an extremely elegant (and dressy) vessel, and culture buffs will appreciate the line's variety of on-board entertainment, including a strong programme of classical music, and a varied lecture programme.

Below: *The explorer ship* Bremen, *seen here in Antarctica, combines an ice-hardened hull with luxurious accommodation.*

Holland America Line

Above: *HOLLAND AMERICA's 55,000grt* Maasdaam *dwarfed by the Alaskan mountains.*

The original *Rotterdam*, launched in 1872, was the first vessel of the Netherlands America Steamship Line – a distinguished company that became known simply as Holland America because of its prolific transatlantic crossings. Now on its sixth *Rotterdam*, Holland America Line still offers a tradition of excellence, although nowadays concentrating on holidaymakers in search of wildlife rather than immigrants in search of the New World. Alaska and the Caribbean are HAL strongholds, with Alaskan shoreside operations conducted by Westours, a corporate subsidiary. Other itinerararies include Hawaii, the Mediterranean, northern Europe and *Rotterdam's* world cruise.

Traditionally synonymous with elegance rather than glitz and discreet good service rather than ostentation, Holland America has always claimed a well-heeled, mature clientele. Since its 1988 take-over by the Carnival Corporation (which also included the HAL subsidiary, Windstar Cruises) it is also increasingly attracting a younger market, especially on Alaskan sailings, and is further broadening its appeal with additional children's facilities. Manned by Dutch officers and boasting Dutch shipping memorabilia, antiques and food specialities, the line also hints at its heritage while remaining firmly ensconsed in the upper levels of mainstream American-style cruising.

The current Holland America fleet can be divided into four ship styles – the mid-sized *Nieuw Amsterdam* and *Noordam* (launched in 1983 and 1984); the large *Westerdam* (1986); the slightly larger *Statendam* (1993), *Maasdam* (1993), *Ryndam* (1994) and *Veendam* (1996); and the largest of the line-up the 62,000grt *Rotterdam VI* (1997). Excellent fitness facilities, varied entertainment,

SHOPPING AT SEA

Most cruise ships provide on-board shopping facilities, ranging from a single retail outlet to a complete mall. Basic necessities, souvenir and logo items, works of art, fashions (including formal wear), gifts and, of course, duty free goods can all be purchased on the high seas. Lines such as CELEBRITY and ROYAL CARIBBEAN even offer a dinner jacket (tuxedo) rental service.

spacious accommodations, extensive buffets and well-organized shore excursions are an integral part of a Holland America cruise.

Intercruise

This Greek cruise company offers a series of lively Mediterranean itineraries aboard the vintage 11,000grt vessel, *La Palma*. Catering to a predominantly European clientele, *La Palma* offers basic, fun-in-the-sun cruising ideally suited to families and young adults on a budget.

Jadrolinjia Cruises

Marketed to a mostly German-speaking clientele, this Croatian line operates the *Dalmacija* (1965) – a diminutive vessel offering modestly priced cruises in Mediterranean waters. Ideally suited to first-time budget cruisers, this ship boasts a relatively low passenger carry (around 300), single-sitting dining and a friendly, intimate ambience.

Using On-Board Telephone and Fax

Any calls you make within the ship (cabin to cabin, to reception etc.) will be free, but if you phone or fax to another vessel or ashore via the ship's satellite, standard charges are around US$15 per minute. If you want to call home, use mobile or public phones in your ports of call. Many calling stations in popular cruise ports accept US dollars as well as local currency for telephone cards. Members of the ship's crew are normally well acquainted with phoning home from the various ports of call on a ship's itinerary, and should be able to advise you on the best way to do it.

Japan Cruise Line (Nippon Cruise Kyakusen)

Catering to both the Japanese corporate and leisure markets, Japan Cruise Line (JCL) operates the *Orient Venus*, an attractive mid-sized vessel launched in 1990. Her sister is the smaller, older *New Utopia* – destined to be superceded by JCL's impressive new 720-passenger vessel launched in 1998. Boasting excellent conference facilities, spacious lounges and accommodations, JCL ships follow extensive itineraries through Southeast Asia.

Leisure Cruises

Having acquired the petite ex-Costa ship, *Daphne*, and renamed her *Switzerland*, this Swiss-based company offers both a range of port-intensive Mediterranean and northern European itineraries, and an extensive 146-day world cruise. *Switzerland* is a vintage 400-passenger ship, providing a comfortable, as opposed to sophisticated, ambience and catering to an international clientele. Sometimes escorted by expert lecturers, her occasionally off-beat destinations will appeal to serious sightseers. Leisure Cruises – marketed in the UK by Voyages Jules Verne – also operates the tall sail ship, *Druzhba*, and a fleet of European riverboats (*see* Chapter 7).

Opposite: *A nautical centrepiece to the glittering atrium on* HOLLAND AMERICA*'s* Statendam.

Louis Cruise Lines

This Cyprus-based cruise line is a subsidiary of the island's major travel and tourism company, the Louis Organization, and as such, its cruises are marketed almost entirely to European (and especially British) vacationers in Cyprus. Four Princesas ships currently fly the Louis flag – the *Princesa Marissa* and *Princesa Cypria* are of ferry design (and still take cars on certain crossings), while the *Princesa Amorosa* and *Princesa Victoria* are purpose-built cruise ships. Sailing out of Limassol on cruises of between two and seven days to Egypt, Israel and Greece and its islands, these ships offer a very basic, port-intensive cruise experience. They do, however, provide good value for money, with shore excursions included in the fare.

Mabuhay Holiday Cruises

Mabuhay's attractively refurbished *Mabuhay Sunshine* carries up to 234 passengers on short island-hopping cruises out of Manila. A contemporary vessel with reasonable leisure facilities and a conference centre, she is targeted at the largely untapped domestic market. But with future itineraries set to include ports of historical and cultural interest as well as popular beach stops, these cruises could also be of wider appeal.

Mar Line

Mar Line's lively *Vistamar*, a modern vessel carrying approximately 300 passengers, is a stylish and intimate ship with single sitting dining, a bubbly nightlife and affordable prices. Attracting mainly Spanish-speaking passengers, the ship's itineraries take it throughout the Mediterranean and South America.

FESTIVALS AND LOCAL HOLIDAYS

You may deliberately plan your cruise to co-incide with a particular event (such as Rio de Janeiro's Carnival in February), but if not remember that during local festivals shoreside services – including taxis and public transport – are likely to be suspended, infrequent and more expensive. A more frequent frustration is arriving in a port on a national holiday or religious day (such as a Sunday). It may be business as usual for the restaurants and shops in tourist zones, but banks, museums and other facilities could be closed.

COMMONLY ASKED CRUISING QUESTIONS (7)

Q: *Can I take my pet with me on a cruise?*
A: Animals are not generally allowed on passenger ships. Notable exceptions are the *Queen Elizabeth 2*, which has an on-board kennels and also takes cats and birds, and certain cargo-passenger ships, such as CURNOW SHIPPING's *RMS St Helena*. Guide dogs may be permitted on board, subject to individual cruise line policies and local quarantine regulations.

Mediterranean Shipping Cruises (MSC)

The passenger division of the giant Mediterranean Shipping Company operates several traditional, mid-sized ships catering to an international mix of passengers, with Italians predominating. The MSC fleet currently comprises the comfortable *Rhapsody* and *Melody*, as well as the vintage *Symphony* and *Monterey*. The fleet is marked by an informal, genial, genuine Italian atmosphere and competitively priced itineraries concentrating on port-intensive tours of the Mediterranean, Caribbean and South America.

Metro Holdings

Singapore-based Metro Holdings (who also trade under the name Sun Cruises) entered the rapidly expanding Southeast Asian market in 1997 with *Sun Vista*, formerly Celebrity's *Meridian*. A mature, well-appointed vessel of some 30,000grt, *Sun Vista* offers a mid-priced, fun cruise with entertainment ranging from nightly cabaret to karaoke and western and Asian dining options which include 24-hour room service and a Japanese restaurant. The ship follows a continuous route between Singapore, Penang, Phuket and Kuala Lumpur.

Below: *The sparkling showroom on METRO HOLDING's* Sun Vista.

Mitsui O.S.K. Passenger Line

A subsidiary of one of the oldest and largest freight shipping companies in the world, the Mitsui O.S.K. Passenger Line (commonly abbreviated to MOPAS) currently operates three mid-sized vessels. *Fuji Maru* (1989) boasts excellent conference facilities and is frequently under corporate charter; *Nippon Maru* – a year younger but of comparable size (22,000grt) – and the smaller (17,000grt) and older (1972) *Shin Sakura Maru* undertake publicly sponsored youth 'friendship cruises' and corporate training trips, along with conventional mid-priced cruises. With a senior, almost exclusively Japanese clientele, they offer a number of traditional features and both Japanese and French cuisine. Itineraries include the Japanese islands, Southeast Asia, Australia, Alaska and a full world cruise.

Above: *NYK's stylish and superbly equipped* Asuka.

NYK (Nippon Yusen Kaisha) Cruises

A subsidiary of NYK Line – one of the world's major shipping companies and parent of American-based Crystal Cruises – NYK Cruises operates the beautiful *Asuka*, launched in 1991. A luxury 584-passenger vessel aimed at the Japanese market, she has all-outside suites (35 per cent with private balconies) and exquisitely furbished public rooms. A sushi bar, Japanese-style spa, *washitu* (room with tatami mats), conference rooms and restaurants serving both Japanese and French cuisine are all featured. *Asuka's* itineraries include Asia (sailing around the Japanese archipelago), the South Pacific (Guam, Australia and New Zealand) and a full global circumnavigation.

New Century Cruise Lines

Singapore-based New Century operates the mid-sized *Leisure World* (formerly NCL's *Skyward*) on year-round Southeast Asian itineraries which include places such as Malacca and Kukup. Catering to a predominantly local clientele, this contemporary, well-appointed ship is aimed at those who enjoy gambling facilities, karaoke and a party atmosphere in comfortable surroundings at affordable prices.

PRIVATE BALCONIES

Private balconies are very much in vogue, even for mid-grade cabins, and while they can be wonderful for private – including nude – sunbathing, you could still be affected by noise or smoke drifting over from your neighbours. Balconies towards the front of the ship may offer the best views, but when the ship is at full speed they can also be very, very windy. Note also that balcony space is sometimes at the expense of cabin space, so that cheaper cabins without a balcony may, in fact, offer more interior space than those with a balcony.

THE NORWAY

The oldest and largest (76,000grt) ship in NCL's fleet is the stately *Norway* – formerly *France* and the star of the former French Line. Launched in 1962, this *grand dame* is one of the very few remaining great ocean liners and is still the world's longest cruise ship. A little surprisingly, considering the limitations of her deep draft in shallow waters, the *Norway* is employed year-round in the Caribbean. She boasts all the amenities one might expect from a classic vessel of this size and is noted for her theme cruises. Music lovers in particular are well-catered for with themes such as the famous annual jazz cruise featuring some of the world's most eminent musicians.

Nina Cruise Line

This Italian company operates the *Italia Prima*, launched in 1948 and one of the oldest ships with a full working itinerary. She has an infamous past for, as the *Stockholm*, she rammed and sank the magnificent liner *Andrea Doria* in 1956. She offers primarily European and Caribbean itineraries for up to 600 passengers and boasts distinctive features such as a Turkish bath and private spa baths in many of the cabins.

Norwegian Cruise Line (NCL)

Founded in 1966, this line has undergone some major changes in recent years, taking over ships of the dismantled Royal Cruise Line and Majesty Cruise Line, and re-structuring and re-naming its fleet. NCL's flagship is the graceful *Norway* (*see* Box), which is supported by a fleet of contemporary mid-sized to large vessels sailing predominantly in the Caribbean, Alaska, Europe, the US east coast and Bermuda. These include the lively *Leeward* (1980); the stylish *Norwegian Crown* and sporty *Norwegian Sea* (formerly *Seaward*), both launched in 1988; and the spacious *Norwegian Dream* (formerly *Dreamward*) and *Norwegian Wind* (formerly *Windward*) respectively launched in 1992 and 1993 and each 'stretched' in 1998 to add more facilities and accommodation. The latter two ships are complemented by two attractive new sisters – the mid-sized *Norwegian Majesty* (formerly Majesty Cruise Line's *Royal Majesty*) and *Norwegian Dynasty* (formerly Cunard's *Crown Dynasty*) also launched in 1993 and 1992 respectively. NCL also intends further expansion, including a new 2000-passenger ship for launch in 1999.

Below: *NCL's* Norway.

The official cruise line of the American National Basketball Association and National Football League Players Association, NCL

Above: Marco Polo *in Antarctica.*

boasts excellent sports and fitness facilities and hosts regular sporting theme cruises. Other themes – most notably, different styles of music – feature heavily in the line's programming.

Orient Lines

Founded in 1992 by the British entrepreneur, Gerry Herrod, Orient Lines operates the stately, 850-passenger *Marco Polo* (1966) on a series of worldwide destination-orientated cruises. With an ice-hardened hull, helipad and ten Zodiac dinghies, this elderly but extensively refurbished vessel successfully doubles as an explorer ship and traditional cruise ship. In this way, she offers the best of both worlds – in-depth lectures, off-beat sightseeing and expeditions, interspersed with cocktail parties, elegant evenings and mainstream cruise comforts and facilities.

P&O Cruises

Founded in the 1830s by Arthur Anderson and Brodie Wilcox, the Peninsular & Oriental Steam Navigation Company – known by all as P&O – is one of the world's oldest and largest lines and parent company of the massive Princess Cruises.

Following the much-lamented retirement of the popular *Canberra*, the line's most celebrated ship is now the *Oriana* – named after a famous predecessor and hinting at its ancestry with the Thackeray Room, Lords Tavern bar and the traditional and plush Theatre Royal. A contemporary 69,000grt vessel, *Oriana* provides facilities and entertainment to appeal to all generations, including good provisions for children. She is joined by the large, well-appointed *Arcadia* (formerly *Star Princess*) and the older, 28,000grt *Victoria* on a variety of itineraries around the Mediterranean, northern Europe and the Caribbean.

CHILDREN'S CLUBS

An increasing attraction in the cruising world is free membership to shipboard children's clubs. CARNIVAL, for example, operates a summer camp-style programme called 'Camp Carnival', while NCL'S 'Circus at Sea' allows participants to try their hand at juggling and other skills, culminating in an end-of-cruise performance.

THE INNOCENTS ABOARD

P&O made a notable literary impact in the nineteenth century with both William Makepeace Thackeray and Mark Twain inspired to write about their time at sea on board P&O ships in their respective books, *From Cornhill to Grand Cairo* (1844) and *The Innocents Abroad* (1869).

How Posh

P&O was, of course, synonymous with colonial travel in the days of the Raj, and merged with the British India Company in 1914. The word 'posh' supposedly derives from this period, being an acronym of Port Out, Starboard Home – the cabin allocation preferred by those who could afford to have a choice on voyages between Britain and India, thus guaranteeing shade from the tropical sun on both legs. As a reminder of its heritage, P&O runs the P.O.S.H. Club for its large numbers of faithful repeat passengers.

Victoria also ventures up the Amazon, while *Oriana* and *Arcadia* both offer full world cruises.

Although unlikely to appeal to those seeking a very upscale, glitzy or cosmopolitan style of cruise, this line is a long-time favourite with British families and mature singles and couples. With regular sailings 'Down Under' and the repositioning of Princess Cruises' *Fair Princess* to Sydney (to replace the popular *Fairstar*), P&O also has a loyal following in Australia and New Zealand.

Paradise Cruises

Competing in the popular Cyprus-Egypt-Israel 'mini cruise' marketplace, Paradise operates the *Atalante* – a vintage mid-sized ship offering lively, fun cruising at competitive prices. Often combined with hotel packages, these budget breaks are unlikely to appeal to sophisticated seasoned cruisers, but are ideally suited to holidaymakers in Cyprus wanting to visit Cairo, the Pyramids and Jerusalem as an extension of their land-based vacation.

Phoenix Reisen

Operating a fleet of comfortable, small and mid-sized older ships, this German-based company offers itineraries that include two full world cruises every year. The 600-passenger *Maxim Gorki* (easily-identifed by its unusual smokestack) and 750-passenger *Albatros* are the largest ships in the fleet at 25,000grt apiece, while the 7000grt *Carina* and 4500grt *Regina Maris* carry 200 and 170 passengers respectively. The fleet offers a convivial, as opposed to a sophisticated, cruise experience, with some fascinating, port-intensive itineraries including the Mediterranean, Red Sea (visiting Yemen and Jordan), Arabian Sea and Gulf (visiting Bahrain, the Emirates and Kuwait), the west and east coasts of Africa, and northern Europe (visiting Greenland, Iceland and Spitzbergen). *Maxim Gorki* and *Albatros* also offer world cruises which visit Central America, the Caribbean, Australia, the South Pacific and some less-frequented ports in the Southeast Asia and the Far East region.

Premier Cruises

Brought together following Premier's recent merger with Dolphin and Seawind cruise lines, Premier's *SeaBreeze*, *OceanBreeze* and *IslandBreeze* are characterful mid-sized ships, launched in 1958, 1955 and 1962 respectively but recently upgraded. Specializing in the 'fun cruise' market, they offer east-coast sailings out of New York, Panama Canal itineraries out of Jamaica and cruises to the Bahamas and eastern and western Caribbean from Miami. Families are well-catered for with children's programmes and appearances by Hanna-Barbera characters such as the Flintstones and Yogi Bear; music fans will enjoy the line's regular themes – ranging from Country and Western to Motown; and singles, young couples and first-timers on a budget might also appreciate the convivial ambience of these action-packed, competitively priced cruises.

The Premier fleet also includes the *Oceanic*, which, with its bright red hull, has entered the competitive Florida family cruising market, and a recent addition, the *Rembrandt* (formerly *Rotterdam*), which will offer itineraries on the Brazilian coast. The oldest member of the Premier stable is the former *Vasco da Gama* (1961), now upgraded and known as *Seawind Crown*, which offers Caribbean itineraries out of Aruba. These can be combined or amalgamated with pre- or post-cruise packages in Aruba, Dominica or St Lucia, and include special wedding packages.

Above: *East meets west – the* Maxim Gorki *entering New York past the Statue of Liberty.*

Opposite: *The Riviera Pool on P&O's* Oriana, *one of three on board.*

CRUISE SUMMIT

The *Maxim Gorki* has the claim to fame of being the venue for the 1989 Malta Summit meeting between US President George Bush and USSR leader Mikhail Gorbachev.

Right: *The elegant interior of the 1995-launched* Sun Princess.

GRAND PRINCESS

The queen of the PRINCESS line is the 105,000grt *Grand Princess* – a vessel too large to transit the Panama Canal. Boasting three show lounges (each giving passengers simultaneous entertainment options), five swimming pools, interactive golf and video technology, a 24-hour restaurant, business centre, wedding chapel and one of the largest casinos at sea, this ship is a fore-runner in offering state-of-the-art facilities. It even houses a spectacular 15-deck-high nightclub reached by a glass-enclosed moving walkway, an health spa with suspended pool and cruising's first motion-based, virtual reality theatre. Launched in 1998 as the largest passenger vessel in the world, *Grand Princess* is the shape of ships to come.

Princess Cruises

P&O's large American-based subsidiary, Princess Cruises, is one of the undisputed leaders of cruising's vast upper-middle market. Named after *Princess Patricia* – the company's first 6000grt vessel – back in 1965, Princess was acquired by P&O in 1974. Shortly afterwards, the line introduced millions of viewers to the idea of taking a cruise when its vessels starred in the long-running television series, *The Love Boat*, which was shown in 93 countries worldwide and is still synonymous with Princess today.

With vessels covering every major cruising region and a stronghold in Alaska and the Caribbean, Princess's strength is traditional, American-style, mainstream cruising. Young families will appreciate the children's facilities, fitness fans will enjoy the 'Cruisercise' programmes; the pizzerias are always a favourite; and the production shows are not only spectacular, but among the most innovative at sea.

The fleet is now divided into the remaining original 'Loveboats' which attract a more senior clientele, and the larger new additions, appealing particularly to families and young couples. The *Pacific-* and *Island Princess* are the oldest (1970/71) and smallest (20,000grt) of the Princess ships, lacking many of the facilities of their glitzier counterparts but following some of the most exciting itineraries; the *Royal-* and *Sky Princess* (both 1984) represent the maturing mid-range of the fleet, carrying up to 1200 passengers apiece; the 70,000grt *Crown-* and *Regal Princess*, with their distinctive dolphin-like observation domes, are the first of the line's real megaships; and the huge *Grand Princess* (*see* Box) and the ultra-modern *Sun-*, *Dawn-* and *Sea Princess* are the giants that epitomize contemporary cruise ship design.

Babysitting Services

Babysitting facilities are offered at a nominal rate by various lines, and P&O's *Oriana* also provides an in-cabin baby-listening facility. Even on those ships that do not officially provide baby-sitters, you may be able to negotiate the services of a volunteer crew member (such as an off-duty stewardess) for a small hourly fee. Ask the Cruise Director's or Purser's staff for details.

Radisson Seven Seas Cruises

This luxury fleet was formed in 1995 with the amalgamation of Diamond Cruises (affiliated to the Radisson Hotel group) and Seven Seas Cruise Line (owned by the Japanese 'K' Line). Operating three diminutive vessels, Radisson Seven Seas is ideally suited to those seeking a sophisticated, low-key, intimate ambience and relatively off-beat destinations. All-outside suites, open sitting dining, watersports facilities and inclusive drinks, gratuities and shore excursions are features of this up-market line.

The largest of the fleet – and one of the world's most unusual-looking cruise ships – is a 20,000grt catamaran, *Radisson Diamond*. Launched in 1992, this 350-passenger vessel boasts light, elegant lounges and dining options that include a splendid main restaurant and Italian trattoria. Although unlikely to appeal to purists, the ship's unique design, together with computer-controlled stabilizers, also makes this an extremely spacious and stable vessel. She is a familiar visitor to ports throughout the Mediterranean and northern Europe and regularly transits the Panama Canal travelling between Costa Rica and Caribbean waters.

Below: *Two hulls of luxury and innovation – the* Radisson Diamond.

The smaller, sleeker *Song of Flower* carries 180 passengers in equally modern, elegant surroundings. Following a variety of trails through Europe and Asia, this yacht-like vessel also provides an extensive topical lecture programme. The launch of the 320-passenger

Paul Gauguin in 1998 brings another dimension to the line's itineraries. Purpose-designed for Polynesia, this light, luxury ship offers a more casual style of cruise. Again, lecture programmes and facilities provide a cultural background to exotic ports such as Tahiti, Bora Bora and Moorea.

Regal Cruises

Founded in 1993 when two travel companies bought the mid-sized 40-year old *Caribe I* from Commodore Cruises and renamed it *Regal Empress*, Regal offers some of the lowest rates in the business. Traditionalists might feel that the classic features of this lovely vintage vessel – including bullion-pane windows and original wood panelling – are somewhat wasted on the line's 'cheap and cheerful' sailings, but such cruises keep her afloat and are certainly a hit with the party crowd. Regal's two to six-day itineraries out of Florida or New York include Key West, Cozumel, Playa del Carmen, Grand Cayman, Jamaica, Bermuda, the Bahamas and New England.

Renaissance Cruises

The only line to number, as opposed to name, its ships, this relatively young company (founded in 1989) has always been synonymous with the luxury niche of the market. It is currently, however, in the process of selling its fleet of eight almost-identical *bijou* vessels as part of a broader long term strategy. The 1998 launch of the first of four 690-passenger ships may be rued by small ship affectionados, but they boast equally spacious accommodations (66 per cent with private balconies) and increased facilities that include six dining options, a spa and business centre.

With little in the way of organized activities or entertainment, these vessels are ideal for those seeking an unstructured, elegantly casual cruise at a competitive price. Pre- and post-cruise land packages are strongly featured and itineraries in the Mediterranean, the Baltic, Indian Ocean and Indonesia look set to be supplemented or superseded by the South Pacific and Caribbean.

BETTER BY HALF

ROYAL CARIBBEAN's *Song of Norway* was the first cruise ship to be 'stretched'. This entailed a visit to a shipyard, where it was cut in half and a new mid-section was inserted to lengthen the ship – an experiment that is now standard practice throughout the industry.

Above: *By setting the funnel well aft,* ROYAL CARIBBEAN'S Grandeur of the Seas *has room for a particularly spacious upper deck and pool area.*

Royal Caribbean International (RCI)

Originally founded in 1969 by three prominent Norwegian companies, Miami-based Royal Caribbean International (known until recently as Royal Carribean Cruise Line) launched its first ship, *Song of Norway*, in 1970, built specifically to sail Caribbean waters, where she was joined by *Nordic Prince* (later sold to Airtours) and *Sun Viking*.

Following the success of these ships, a new generation of Royal Caribbean vessels was introduced with the *Song of America*. She was to pave the way for the 2300-passenger *Sovereign of the Seas*, *Monarch of the Seas* and *Majesty of the Seas* – a trio that gave the line the claim to fame of being the first company to operate three passenger ships in excess of 70,000grt. Now firmly established as one of the industry's major players (and having recently acquired Celebrity Cruises), Royal Caribbean has rapidly expanded its fleet to include the equally king-sized *Legend-*, *Splendour-*, *Grandeur-*, *Rhapsody-*, *Enchantment-* and *Vision of the Seas*. These vessels offer a wealth of facilities, entertainment and diversions, including children's programmes, conference centres, impressive fitness facilities, hi-tech production shows and cruising's first ever 18-hole miniature golf courses.

CARIBBEAN CHARM

RCI's stronghold in the Caribbean means that passengers have exclusive access to Crown & Anchor Clubs (named after the line's distinctive logo) in **St Thomas** and **Puerto Rico**, and use of the private islands of Labadee and Cococay as day resorts.

Greece is the Word

Lovers of all things Greek will enjoy themselves on Royal Olympic ships – Syrtaki dancing, Greek nights, on-board tavernas, speciality Greek dishes, Greek officers and dining room staff are integral features of a cruise. Another feature of their ships is a fascinating 'Olympic Corner', displaying memorabilia and artefacts from the ancient and modern Olympic Games.

Royal Hispania Cruises

Operating the small, 10,000grt *Don Juan* (1967) in Mediterranean waters, Royal Hispania offers lively Spanish-style cruising, including – somewhat unusually – mainly Spanish officers. Providing a comfortable as opposed to sophisticated cruise experience, this vessel is well-suited to those looking for port-intensive itineraries and a cheery cosmopolitan atmosphere.

Royal Olympic Cruises

In December 1995, two established Greek lines, Epirotiki and Sun Line, merged to form Royal Olympic Cruises. By concentrating on familiar waters, the combined fleets now have a stronghold at the economy to mid-priced end of the Mediterranean cruising market, with attractive port-intensive itineraries that also extend to the Black Sea and northern Europe. Notable features of Royal Olympic cruises are visits to lovely, less-frequented Greek islands, raw tourist destinations such as Albania and transits of the Corinth and Kiel canals.

The Royal Olympic fleet comprises the *Stella Solaris, Stella Oceanis, Orpheus, Triton, Odysseus* and *Olympic*. With sizes ranging from 5500grt to 31,500grt and launch dates from 1952 to 1971, these vessels are in a different league to the huge new megaships, but they do provide a convivial, Mediterranean ambience in traditional surroundings. The character of the ships changes according to the season, with families in the summertime, seniors in the winter and the stately *Stella Solaris*, in particular, attracting a year-round clientele of repeat passengers.

Royal Seas Cruise Line

This recently formed company offers short breaks out of Tampa to the Caribbean and coast of Mexico aboard the *Royal Seas* (1975). A mid-sized vessel, she hosts competitively priced cruises suited to those seeking a comfortable 'party ship' with an unpretentious, lively ambience and sunny destinations.

Opposite: *The opulent main lounge on* Seabourn Spirit, *where everything stops for tea.*

Saga Holidays

The Saga Group has long marketed cruises to the over 50s, so it was a logical step when the company acquired the aptly named *Sagafjord* from Cunard in 1996. Renamed *Saga Rose*, this grand old lady offers one of cruising's most varied yearly programmes, including the Caribbean, Mediterranean, Baltic and Arctic Circle and a full world cruise in the spring.

Saga Rose offers a very traditional cruise experience, with single sitting dining, spacious public rooms and elegantly tiered aft decks. Sailing out of Dover in the UK, she is perhaps the only cruise ship in the world to specify 50 as a lower age limit! Many of her clientele have cruised previously and appreciate the high crew to passenger ratio and inclusive insurance and gratuities.

NOISY CABINS

Irrespective of grade, be wary of cabins marked next to unmarked spaces on the ship plan, as these may represent crew stairwells or noisy pantries. Such cabins will be known to shipboard personnel as 'disadvantaged', even though they may cost exactly the same as others in the same rank. Naturally, they are best avoided, but if you have no choice in your allocation and are genuinely disturbed by noise or other factors, air your grievance to the purser or berthing officer as early as possible in the cruise. Unless the ship is full, they should – and usually, will – do their best to re-accommodate you.

Seabourn Cruise Line

Anchored firmly at the exclusive end of the market, *Seabourn Pride*, *Seabourn Spirit* and *Seabourn Legend* each provide open sitting dining, opulently spacious accommodations and facilities that include a rear watersports marina, spa, gymnasium, casino and business centre. With a mere 200 passengers each, activities and entertainment tend to be deliberately low-key, comprising evening cabarets, live music for dancing, special interest lectures or celebrity chef demonstrations.

Jointly owned by the line's founder, Atle Brynestad, and the giant Carnival Corporation, Seabourn pampers its clientele with some unique touches, including personalized stationery and 'His and Hers' coloured bathroom towels. Although offering a high level of service (and 24-hour room service), a no tipping policy is also enforced.

THE SILVERSEA EXPERIENCE

SILVERSEAS' unusual worldwide itineraries include extensive cruising in the East and South China Seas and visits to less-common passenger ports such as Northern Ireland's Belfast and Londonderry. On all cruises, inclusive 'Silversea Experience' shore excursions are designed to show passengers memorable, and often unique, cultural events or locations.

Siam Cruise

This Thai company offers cruises in the waters of the Gulf of Thailand and around Malaysia to the Andaman Sea aboard the 5000grt *Andaman Princess*. A traditional vessel launched in 1962, which caters predominantly to a Thai and Malaysian clientele, *Andaman Princess* offers a basic, destination-orientated cruise.

Silversea Cruises

Smaller than the ships of Crystal Cruises and more competitively priced than Seabourn, Silversea competes in the same up-market niche of the cruise market. Founded in 1992, this line is 'always exclusive, all inclusive' – a motto referring as much to the company's no tipping policy and inclusive beverages as its sophisticated cruising lifestyle.

The fleet comprises the elegant sisters, *Silver Cloud* and *Silver Wind*, launched in 1994 and 1995 respectively. With a passenger carry of 296, these ships can still offer a relatively intimate cruise experience, but with more amenities and entertainment than some of their yacht-like competitors. Open sitting dining, 24-hour room service, a health spa, watersports platform and attractive show lounge are integral features. In addition, an affiliation with Le Cordon Bleu culinary academy has resulted in menus, demonstrations and wine-tastings of real appeal to gourmets, and unusual itineraries (*see* Box) also make for an original cruise experience. The 1998 and 1999 launch of the fleet's second set of 'twins', each accommodating up to 390 passengers, promises an even greater diversity of itineraries.

CONGRATULATIONS!

Let the cruise line know if your birthday, wedding anniversary or honeymoon coincides with your vacation, and you may well receive a cake at dinner – and perhaps a bottle of sparkling wine – and be serenaded by an enthusiastic, if not entirely tuneful, troupe of minstrel waiters. (If you do *not* want this to happen, also let the cruise line know.)

Special treatment is also reserved for faithful past passengers, such as members of PRINCESS CRUISES' Captain's Circle, P&O's P.O.S.H. Club or CRYSTAL CRUISES' Crystal Society. These clubs commonly offer generous discounts or priority booking, an invitation to a private on-board cocktail party, a copy of a special magazine or various pins and logo items.

Spice Island Cruises

The lovely little ships of Spice Island Cruises ply the waters of Indonesia, offering a glimpse of some of the region's less visited islands as well as major tourist destinations. The 140-passenger *Bali Sea Dancer* is a characterful older ship with attractive traditional Indonesian decor, while the modern *Oceanic Odyssey* (formerly Showa Line's *Oceanic Grace*) is a deluxe

120-passenger vessel more akin to a private yacht. Both ships offer single sitting dining, live music for dancing, a swimming pool, gymnasium, beauty salon, boutique and library. *Oceanic Odyssey* also has a dedicated jogging track, male and female saunas, jacuzzi and a specially configured suite for disabled passengers.

Above: *The colourful Indonesian-style interior of* Bali Sea Dancer.

Sailing out of Bali, the line's three- and four-night itineraries regularly include Komodo, Sumbawa (Badas and Bima) and Lombok. Highlights include snorkelling and diving around the region's coral reefs (including the services of certified dive masters), escorted flora and fauna discovery trips, visits to local villages and cultural displays. Between November and April, *Oceanic Odyssey* also ventures around the islands and Asmat areas of Irian Jaya, the Great Barrier Reef, the South Pacific (including Fiji) and coastal New Zealand.

Star Cruise

Singapore-based Star Cruise is one of the fastest-expanding new lines on the block, with *SuperStar Virgo* the eighth vessel to be introduced since the company's formation in 1993. Already the largest cruise line in Asia, it is rapidly becoming one of the largest in the world.

The fleet is actually divided into three categories – Star, SuperStar and MegaStar – each offering ships of a different size or style. *Star Aquarius* and *Star Pisces* are the company's original large, hi-density (1900 passenger capacity) budget-cruise ships with excellent children's facilities, while *MegaStar Aries* and *MegaStar Taurus* are – in contrast to their names – petite luxury yacht-like vessels, often privately chartered and each with a crew of 80 for the 72 guests. The SuperStar category consists of the mid-sized *SuperStar Gemini*, the *SuperStar Capricorn* and two real 'SuperStars', due for launch in 1998 and 1999 – *SuperStar Leo* and *SuperStar Virgo*. These huge floating

BLACKENED IN THE SUN

Sun decks which are positioned towards the stern of a cruise ship might be sheltered from the wind, but they are prone to showers of soot from the ship's funnel. Never sit on a sun lounger or chair in these areas without first inspecting it – especially if you're wearing white!

COMMONLY ASKED CRUISING QUESTIONS (8)

Q: *What if I miss the ship?*
A: If you miss the ship (because of flight delays etc.) and you are on a fly/cruise package, the airline and/or cruise line representatives will take full responsibility for getting you to the vessel. The same applies if you are on one of the ship's organized excursions. If you are joining the ship or sightseeing independently, however, you will be personally responsible if you miss the boat.

If you do find yourself watching the ship sail without you, get in touch with the appropriate shipping agency straight away. Contact information for the agent (together with 'All Aboard' and sailing times) may be listed in your Daily Programme. It may be possible to hitch a lift with the pilot boat, or the agent may assist with arrangements to join the ship at its next port.

resorts each accommodate up to 2800 passengers and feature state-of-the-art leisure and entertainment facilities – including a public observation area with video monitors which explain the technical workings of the ship.

Sailing almost entirely out of the modern Singapore Cruise Centre (only *Star Pisces* is based in Hong Kong), the fleet is perfectly located for its year-round short cruises to Malaysia, Thailand, China, Taiwan and Japan.

Swan Hellenic Cruises

Acquired by the P&O Group in 1982, Swan Hellenic boasts a heritage that can be traced back to the Hellenic Travel Club in the 1890s. It is now a relatively upmarket line offering winter cruising in the Persian Gulf, Indian Ocean and regions of Southeast Asia and extensive itineraries in northern Europe and the Mediterranean. Having previously chartered Royal Olympic's *Orpheus* for over twenty years, Swan Hellenic now charters the *Minerva* (1996). An elegant, contemporary ship with traditional lines, *Minerva* carries up to 392 passengers and sets out to attract the 'thinking' cruiser with an informal ambience, open sitting dining and engaging yet accessible special interest cruises (*see* Box).

Thomson Cruises

A subsidiary of the largest tour operator in the UK, Thomson Cruises competes head-on with Airtours in the burgeoning British cruise market. It currently offers Mediterranean itineraries out of Mallorca and Cyprus aboard the *Sapphire* and *Emerald* (under charter from Louis Lines) and Florida, the Bahamas and Gulf of Mexico aboard the *Topaz*. Thomson also markets the ships of other lines, including Premier, NCL and Star Cruise.

The 650-passenger *Sapphire* (formerly *Ocean Princess*) is the newest of the Thomson-operated vessels, originally launched in 1967. *Emerald* and *Topaz* are older but larger, boasting passenger capacities of 1153 and 962 apiece. All three are comfortable mid-sized ships catering to the vast market of first-time cruisers, many of whom are recruited from Thomson's ranks of land-based

Above: *SWAN HELLENIC's* Minerva *soaking up the culture in Venice.*

holidaymakers. Not surprisingly, pre- and post-cruise hotel packages are a popular option. *Topaz* also offers all-inclusive drinks and a cabaret restaurant.

Transocean Reederei

Transocean operates the diminutive *Calypso* – a ship launched in 1968 and carrying approximately 500 passengers on relatively off-beat worldwide itineraries. An unpretentious vessel, she is ideally suited to German-speaking cruisers looking for a modestly priced cruise with the focus placed firmly on destinations. Transocean has also recently undertaken the operation of the comparatively younger (1987), larger, less crowded and more up-market *Astor* – an attractive ship of 20,000grt which offers elegant, comfortable cruising to destinations worldwide.

Vergina Cruises

An off-shoot of Piraeus-based Vergina Lines ferry company, Vergina's *Queen Eleni* offers high-density sailing between Greece, Egypt and Israel. With few facilities and spartan accommodations, this type of travel experience cannot reasonably compare with even a mass market cruise, but the attractive port-intensive itinerary might appeal to passengers on a budget and those for whom the destination is the focus.

SPECIAL INTEREST CRUISES ON SWAN HELLENIC

SWAN HELLENIC's *Minerva* is noted for its special interest cruises, featuring an excellent lecture programme and inclusive related shore excursions. Literature, history, art, archaeology, ornithology, marine biology, music and astronomy are among the featured themes, while recent cruise titles have included 'The Celtic West', 'The Arts of Iberia', 'The Romans in Africa' and 'Greece: The Classics'.

6
Where to Cruise

Just as our image of the globe is given definition by the oceans of the world, so much of the world orientates itself by the sea. Sailing across these oceans and seas, between islands and along coastlines, the breadth of coverage of the world's cruise lines is evidence of the potency of travelling the world by sea. Indeed, as anyone who has ever sailed on a ship will testify, there is no better way to arrive in a new place.

The world's most popular cruising region is still very much the **Caribbean**, but in recent years other regions such as **Alaska**, the **Mediterranean** and **northern Europe** have seen a large increase in passenger shipping and the **South Pacific Ocean** looks set to become the cruise destination of the new millennium. This chapter looks in turn at the different major cruising regions of the world and at their most popular ports-of-call, highlighting sights and events of particular interest and appeal to mainstream cruise passengers. For the regions specially covered by explorer, coastal and riverboat cruises, see Chapter 7.

CARIBBEAN: WHEN TO GO

While the Caribbean offers 52-week cruising and consistently high temperatures between 18°C (64°F) and 33°C (91°F), arguably the best time to visit is between **January** and **May**, when the climate is less humid.

Temperatures, humidity and tropical rainfall levels all rise between June and November – the period regarded as the **hurricane** season. Thanks to Christmas holidays, **December** is regarded as peak season, although normally it is not quite as warm as the first months of the new year.

THE CARIBBEAN

Over 50 per cent of cruise ship passengers choose the Caribbean as their playground – and it's easy to see why. Palm-fringed beaches, turquoise waters and sunny skies make for an ideal holiday destination – and with so many beautiful islands within easy sailing of each other, the best way to appreciate the diversity of the region is undoubtedly by sea.

Opposite: *Pidgeon Point in Tobago – another balmy, scenic cruise stop in the Caribbean, the world's most popular cruising region.*

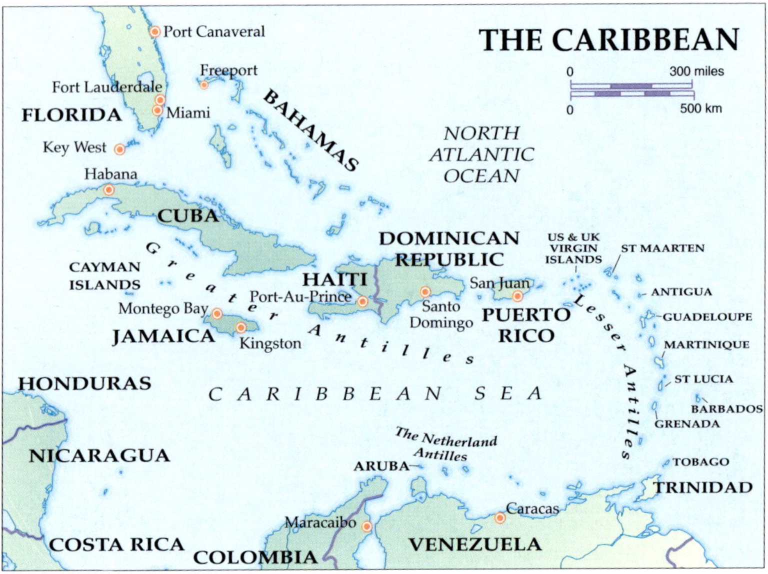

A large number of Caribbean cruises begin and end in **Florida**, utilizing **Miami** and **Port Everglades** (by Fort Lauderdale) as the embarkation ports, although **Port Canaveral**, home of the John F. Kennedy Space Center and close to Disney World, is gaining in popularity. Before sailing on to the Caribbean proper, a number of lines make a stop at **Key West**, the island at the southern tip of Florida where Ernest Hemingway once hung out.

The closest of the Caribbean islands to Florida are the beautiful **Bahamas**, which offer a wide range of activities, from swimming with dolphins at Lucaya to duty-free shopping in Freeport and watching flamingos at Adastra Gardens. Just to the south of the Bahamas are the largest Caribbean islands, including **Cuba**, which shares a rich history with its neigbouring islands, the **Dominican Republic** and its capital **Santo Domingo**, the oldest city in the New World, and **Puerto Rico**, with its quaint old town of **San Juan** and El Yunque rainforest inland. Another north Caribbean favourite is **Jamaica**, home of reggae and the famous Montego Bay.

CARIBBEAN: DON'T MISS

Antigua: Make your way to historic Nelson's Dockyard and English Harbour.
Bahamas: Go swimming with dolphins at Lucaya.
Jamaica: See spectacular Dunn's River Falls.
Miami: Tour the Art Deco District, Miami Beach, and Bayside and Coconut Grove for shopping and dining.
Port Canaveral: Visit Disney World and the John F Kennedy Space Center.
St Lucia: Take a helicopter ride over Les Pitons.
Trinidad: For one of the best carnivals in the world.
Virgin Gorda: Swim in the famous Baths.

Above: *NCL's* Windward *glides out of the historic port of San Juan on the island of Puerto Rico.*

Most of the remaining Caribbean islands are spread out in a sparkling crescent between the Caribbean Sea and the Atlantic Ocean. Almost all boast wonderful beaches, with those of **Antigua**, the idyllic island of **Aruba** in the Netherlands Antilles and the tiny **Grenadines** standing out. On **St Thomas** in the US Virgin Islands, Magen's Bay is consistently voted one of the world's top ten beaches, while on nearby **Virgin Gorda** in the British Virgin Islands the famous Baths are always popular for swimming. Divers can enjoy some spectacular locations, including **Grenada**, **Tobago** and Buck Island Reef – the only underwater national park in the USA – in **St Croix** in the US Virgin Islands, while in the **Cayman Islands** you can snorkel with stingrays at Stingray City. For those who don't snorkel or scuba dive, it is possible to visit underwater observatories (such as the Coral World resorts) or take a glass-bottom boat or submarine trip (on an Atlantis submarine).

Other popular activities include sailing trips in places such as the **British Virgin Islands** or rum cruises aboard vessels such as the *Jolly Roger* (out of **Barbados**). When it comes to **parties** the Caribbean is a past master, and nowhere more so than **Trinidad**, which hosts one of the world's great carnivals. Duty-free shopping is a popular feature of busy islands such as **St Thomas**, **St Maarten** and **Martinique**, as well as more exclusive spots such as **St Barts** and **Curaçao**, home of the famous liqueur.

TAKING CARE IN THE CARIBBEAN

- The crime rate in **Jamaica** is high. Leave valuables on the ship and take taxis or organized excursions rather than walk in the downtown areas. Be prepared to be hassled by vendors of *ganja* (marijuana).
- Taxis in **Martinique** are expensive. Consider walking into town or go with an organized excursion.
- Parts of **San Juan** (Puerto Rico) and **Charlotte Amalie** (in St Thomas in the US Virgin Islands) can be dangerous – especially at night. In the evenings, take taxis to and from the ship.

South and Central America: When To Go

The Mexican Riviera is warm **year-round**, with temperatures almost always between 19°C (66°F) and 33°C (91°F). **October and November** are good off-peak months to visit **Mexico**, avoiding the springtime crowds and tropical summer rains. In contrast, the **South American** cruising season tends to run from **September** until **April**, with temperatures from 8°C (46°F) lows in southern Argentina to 34°C (93°F) highs in Brazil's equatorial Manaus. **September to December** is a drier and less humid time to explore the **Amazon.**

South and Central America

Although not an area of mainstream cruising, South and Central America contains an incredible diversity of nature, culture and shore-side activities. Cruises explore the **Amazon river**, transit **Panama**'s famous canal, visit vibrant cities such as **Buenos Aires**, **Acapulco** and **Rio de Janeiro**, attract archeologists to the remains of ancient civilizations and naturalists to places such as Ecuador's **Galápagos Islands** and **Costa Rica**, while swinging hammocks and cold tequilas tempt those for whom any of the above sounds too much like hard work.

Mexico – and increasingly **Venezuela** and **Colombia** – are often incorporated into regular Caribbean cruises, while **Costa Rica** is a frequent addition to Panama Canal

Left: Regal Princess *making her journey through the Panama Canal, which deserves a place on the 'hit list' of every keen traveller.*

transits. Such itineraries also regularly include the US ports of **San Diego** and **Los Angeles** on the west coast, and **Galveston** and **New Orleans** on the Gulf of Mexico.

The west coast of Mexico is often known as the **Mexican Riviera**, a place where glamorous tourism and rich history mix against the backdrop of a sparkling sea and some stunning coastal scenery. At the base of the Baja California peninsula is **Cabo San Lucas**, where you can see the amazing underwater life in a glass bottom boat ride to Los Arcos, while down the coast are the resorts of **Mazatlán**, **Puerto Vallarta**, **Manzanillo**, **Zihuatanejo** and **Acapulco**, famous for its cliff divers, beaches, hotels and the view of its famous bay.

On the east coast, **Playa del Carmen** offers the chance to visit the Mayan ruins at Tulum or Chitzen Itza, as well as the Sian Ka'an Biosphere Reserve (a World Heritage Site for endangered species), while **Cozumel Island** is a place to dive or snorkel on the local reefs. From **Belize City** you can take the chance to dive on one of the world's longest barrier reefs, while the spectacular natural highlights of **Costa Rica** tend to be inland – such as Braulio Carrillo National Park, accessible from **Puerto Limón**, and Poas Volcano National Park, best reached from **Puerto Caldera** on the Pacific coast, which is also the access point for the capital, **San José**.

Staying Safe in South America

- **Street crime** is a major problem in some South American cities, the obvious example being **Rio de Janeiro**, where it is advisable to take an organized tour or at least a taxi. Don't sport expensive-looking jewellery or cameras and be aware of pickpockets, especially in crowded areas.
- While they are relatively safe and inexpensive, be aware that most **taxis** in **Buenos Aires** only take two passengers.
- Be wary of the quality of the **silver** sold by street traders. Some pieces are guaranteed to turn green by the end of your cruise!

SOUTH AND CENTRAL AMERICA: DON'T MISS

Acapulco (Mexico): See the cliff divers at La Quebrada and shop for silver, rugs and colourful hammocks.
Buenos Aires (Argentina): Tour the city or visit the Iguassu Falls, a gaucho ranch or a tango nightclub.
Cozumel (Mexico): For the Mayan sites of Tulum or Chitzen Itza, and diving on the local reefs.
Guayaquil (Ecuador): A base port for trips to the Galápagos Islands or the mountain city of Quito.
New Orleans (Louisiana, USA): Famous for its Mardi Gras, nostalgic jazz clubs and cajun cooking.
Rio de Janeiro (Brazil): Take the cable-car up Sugar Loaf Mountain for the vista, visit Ipanema and Copacabana beaches or the tropical Tijuca jungle, and don't miss the world's most famous carnival.

South American ports tend to be visited mainly by ships on trans-global voyages, passenger-cargo and explorer vessels. HAPAG-LLOYD's *Hanseatic* follows a particularly far-reaching route and PRINCESS CRUISES is one of the few mainstream lines to offer extensive South American itineraries, covering both east and west coasts. Important ports-of-call include **La Guaira** in Venezuela, the gateway to Caracas and the spectacular Angel Falls, **Fortaleza**, **Recife** and **Salvador de Bahia** on the Brazilian coast, and **Rio de Janeiro**, one of the world's great cruising destinations and the scene of the world's most spectacular carnival.

In Uruguay, **Punte del Este** is a fashionable resort and **Montevideo** is a place to uncover some typical Uruguyan life, while **Buenos Aires**, Argentina's capital, has some important sites and is the gateway to the interior of that country. Certain cruises also visit the remote **Falkland Islands**, home of some unusual wildlife, including the tiny Magallenic penguins which live on Carcass Island.

NORTH AMERICA (EAST COAST)

From South Carolina to the Gulf of St Lawrence, coastal cruising along North America's Atlantic coast provides a scenic alternative to Alaska and a deep insight into American history. As those seeking sun and fun fly south to warmer climes, this area becomes the preserve of 'proper sailors', seafood-connoisseurs and nature-lovers. Graceful scenery and the rich colours of autumn make **New England**, in particular, a popular choice for cruises later in the season.

The US east coast between Florida and New York City is not prime cruising territory, with relatively few good harbours. Those that are visited, however, include **Savannah**, Georgia, **Charleston**, South Carolina and **Williamsburg**, Virginia, all rich in colonial and Civil War history. The only way to arrive in **New York City** is, of course, by sea, sailing past the Statue of Liberty with Manhattan as a backdrop. Further along the New England coast is **Newport**, Rhode Island, host of music

Left: *Quebec City on the St Lawrence Seaway receives a visit from* Crystal Harmony.

festivals and yacht races and the site of some magnificent colonial mansions, while the island of **Nantucket** is a place to explore in laid-back style, by foot or bicycle. The area around **Cape Cod** and **Boston** has plenty to offer, from the city's many arts and sporting attractions to beaches and a Heritage Trail of historic landmarks.

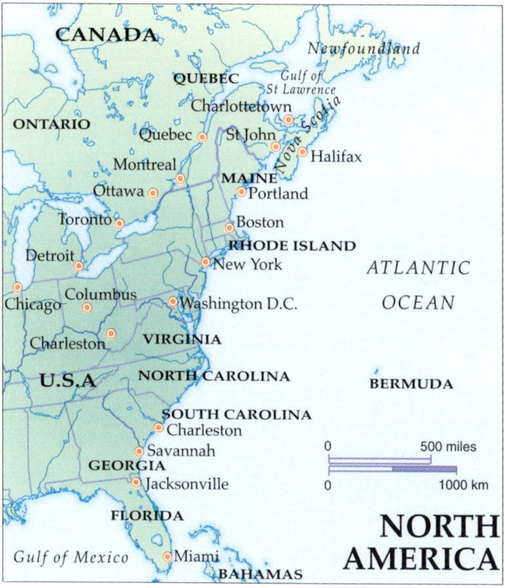

North America: When To Go

Windjammers and coastal vessels as well as regular cruise ships sail here from **May** through to **October** when northeastern temperatures can reach 28°C (82°F) and rarely drop below 10°C (50°F). **July** and **August** are the **warmest** months, although those seeking the spectacular **autumn foliage** should plan their cruise between **mid-September and mid-October**.

Temperatures in **Bermuda** and **south of Philadephia** are proportionately higher, reaching 30°C (86°F) in July and August. In spite of mild winters, few vessels call at Bermuda between November and April .

North American East Coast: Don't Miss

Bermuda: Shop for those special shorts along Hamilton's Front Street or relax on pink sand beaches.
Montreal: Take a horse and carriage (*calèche*) around the pretty old quarter, visit the magnificent Notre Dame Basilica or head for the Laurentian Mountains.
New England: Famous for clam chowder, autumnal colours and boat building.
New York: See the view from the World Trade Center, shop in Bloomingdales, catch a Broadway Show, discover Central Park, Wall Street and Times Square.
Quebec City: Explore the winding streets of this proud walled city, with its military heritage and Citadel.

Above: *Soaking up the sun in Hamilton, Bermuda.*

The coast of **Maine** is all about quaint fishing harbours, traditional seafaring life and great seafood, with itineraries including harbours such as **Portland**, **Boothbay Harbour** and **Rockland**. Along the rugged Canadian coast **Halifax** in Nova Scotia has the Maritime Museum of the Atlantic and a number of coastal wrecks for diving, while **Charlottetown**, Prince Edward Island, is a base for some lovely beaches, fishing villages and PEI National Park.

Down the **St Lawrence Seaway** are the historic centres of **Quebec City** and **Montreal**, while another highlight of the Canadian coast is **St John's** in Newfoundland, where you can see the Signal Hill National Historic Site, the old whaling port of Red Bay and some rugged coastal scenery.

One of the more out-of-the-way highlights in this area is the group of approximately 150 Atlantic islands collectively known as **Bermuda**, some 920 km (570 miles) east of North Carolina's Cape Hatteras. The largest of these, **Great Bermuda**, is cruising's famous pastel-pink island, with three ports of call, Royal Dockyard, Hamilton and St George's.

ALASKA

Despite a relatively brief cruising season, an Alaskan cruise offers spectacular scenery, an abundance of wildlife, fresh bracing air and laid-back, relatively crime-free ports of call. PRINCESS CRUISES and HOLLAND AMERICA LINE have a regional stronghold here that includes extensive shoreside operations (Princess Tours and Westours respectively), but other companies are also heading north to stake their claim in the cruise industry's very own goldrush.

Although restrictions are enforced to limit cruise-ship traffic in this environmentally sensitive part of the world, the range of itineraries is presently expanding beyond the classic **Inside Passage** route to include the **Gulf of Alaska**. Another popular feature of Alaskan cruises are pre- and post-cruise packages in **Anchorage**, **Vancouver**, the **Canadian Rockies** or **Denali National Park**, as well as embarkation ports in the USA such as **Seattle** and **San Francisco**.

Wildlife, including prolific bird- and sea-life, is a highlight of any cruise in this area, along with some spectacular scenery. **Glacier Bay** is still the classic place to see huge glaciers, humpback whales, seabirds, seals and other forms of marine life, although **Tracy Arm Fjord** is less well known but just as impressive. The natural environment also provides a playground for

ALASKA: WHEN TO GO

Weather conditions limit Alaskan cruising to a five month period, **May to September**. Even during these months – and especially early and late season – the climate can be extremely **unpredictable** with rain, mists and glorious sunshine interchanging by the hour. Average temperatures range from 12°C (54°F) in May and September to 17°C (63°F) in July, rarely falling below 3°C (37°F) or rising above 21°C (70°F) during the whole season. **June** can be a particularly pleasant time to visit, before the peak season crowds, although in July and August **mosquitoes** can be a problem – remember to pack the insect repellent.

US AND CANADIAN WEST COAST: WHAT TO SEE

Many Alaskan cruises depart from ports on the North American west coast. Among the highlights are:

San Francisco: Be on deck as you sail under the Golden Gate Bridge. Also look out for Fisherman's Wharf, Chinatown, Nob Hill, Alcatraz and those famous cable-cars!

Vancouver: Sightseeing should include Stanley Park, Grouse Mountain and the Capilano suspended foot-bridge (the world's longest). Be on deck as you sail under the Lion's Gate Bridge.

Victoria: Stroll around this pretty town, with afternoon tea at the Empress Hotel.

Right: *The 70,000grt mega-ship* Regal Princess *noses up to a glacier in Glacier Bay, Alaska.*

exciting **adventure trips**, including kayaking, rafting and jet-boat rides, float plane and helicopter flights over glaciers, and dog-sled rides. The evocative days of the **gold rush** are recounted on the White Pass and Yukon railway at **Skagway**, as well as in Alaska's famous bars, such as the Red Dog Saloon in petite state capital **Juneau** or the Salty Dawg Saloon in **Homer**. For anyone interested in the indigenous culture of the region, the totem poles at Saxman Village at **Ketchikan**, the totem trail through **Sitka**'s beautiful National Historical Park and the petroglyphs (stone markings) near **Wrangell** are all worth checking out.

ALASKA: DON'T MISS

Glacier Bay: Enjoy a memorable day in the company of whales and glaciers.
Juneau: Take a helicopter ride and walk on a glacier.
Skagway: Take the White Pass and Yukon Railway train on a scenic Gold Rush trip, or stroll up the main street with its vintage vehicles, quaint shops and Red Onion Saloon.
Tracy Arm Fjord: Some spectacular scenery to rival that of Glacier Bay.

The Mediterranean and Black Sea

For anyone interested in archaeology, history, languages, good food and art and culture, the Mediterranean region takes some beating. From the chic French Riviera to the sun drenched Greek Islands, the sands of North Africa to the pine-clad banks of the Ukraine, this part of the seafarer's globe offers more cultural diversity than almost any other cruising area.

This is reflected in the conditions and styles of the many vessels that ply these waters and it is advisable to compare what's on offer carefully before booking. European-based or marketed cruise lines regularly 'head for the Med', as do some (particularly up-market) US-based vessels, sailing ships and yachts.

Eastern Mediterranean

The dazzling array of **Greek islands** provides a wonderful venue for cruising, with superb weather and numerous ports of call where you can enjoy food, wine and ancient culture. The list of highlights can feel endless: the famous archeological site of Knossos on **Crete**, the white-washed houses, windmills and beach bars of **Mykonos**, the pretty village of Thira and the artists' village of Oia on **Santorini**, or the Palace and Street of the Knights on **Rhodes**. On the mainland, **Piraeus** is the busy ferry and cruise ship embarkation port for **Athens**, Nauplia is the port for **Epidaurus**, **Corinth** and **Mycenae** – an archaeologist's dream, **Itea** is situated by the site of ancient **Delphi**, while Katakolon and Patras are used as the ports for ancient **Olympia**, home of the Olympic Games.

The most popular cruise spot in the **Adriatic** is

THE MEDITERRANEAN: WHEN TO GO

Weather and sea conditions restrict the main cruising season to the **summer** months (**April to October**), particularly in the Black Sea region. Although some ships offer year-round sailing, most reposition for the winter or at least move westwards. **July and August** are the **hottest** months with highs regularly exceeding 28°C (82°F). **December and January** are the **coolest**, although temperatures rarely drop below 10°C (50°F). The exception to this is the Black Sea area, which is proportionally cooler even in peak summer. **May, June** and **early September** are good months to visit if you wish to avoid the peak temperatures and crowds.

Above: *Slipping past Santorini.*

EASTERN MEDITERRANEAN: DON'T MISS

Santorini (Greece): Ride a donkey (or cable-car) from the harbour to Thira village, or swim in the volcanic crater!
Athens (Greece): See the Acropolis, the district of Plaka and the guards in Constitution Square.
Venice (Italy): Visit St Mark's Square, the Doge's Palace, Bridge of Sighs and 'Bellinis' in Harry's Bar.
Cairo (Egypt): Go for the museums, magnificent mosques and Grand Bazaar, as well as the Pyramids.
Istanbul (Turkey): See the Galata Bridge, Blue Mosque and exotic Grand Bazaar.

Venice, although there are now more unusual stops in this region at **Dubrovnik** in Croatia, where ships are calling again following the Croatia–Serbia conflicts, and **Albania**, a closed country until 1992 and still raw to tourism.

The history and colour are also rich along the **Turkish coast**, with ancient sites, bazaars, beaches, restaurants and bars in places such as **Alanya**, **Antalya**, **Bodrum**, **Marmaris** and **Fethiye**. Along the **Dardanelles** strait between the Aegean and Marmora seas you can spot the British, Commonwealth, French and Turkish World War I memorials, while a stop at Çanakkale allows you to take a ferry to the poignant war memorials and cemeteries of the **Gallipoli** peninsula, as well as visit ancient **Troy**. At **Kusadasi** you can see the site of ancient Ephesus, while there's also a colourful market at **Dikili**, by the ancient ruins at Pergamum.

A number of eastern Mediterranean cruises sail in the **Cyprus–Israel–Egypt** triangle, departing from **Limassol** in Cyprus and calling at **Ashdod** or **Haifa** in Israel, both gateways to **Jerusalem**, and **Alexandria** or **Port Said** in

Egypt, a full-day trip from **Cairo** and Giza's famous Pyramids and Sphinx.

On **Black Sea** itineraries **Istanbul**, one of the world's great ports and the only city in the world to straddle two continents (Europe and Asia), is always a popular stop. Other notable ports-of-call are **Varna** in Bulgaria, where you can visit a local winery or stroll along miles of untamed beaches, **Constanta** in Romania, memorable for its local folk art and music, and the Ukrainian ports of **Odessa**, a place of elegantly decaying architecture and a beautiful opera house, and **Yalta**, site of the White Palace at Livadia where the famous conference between Stalin, Churchill and Roosevelt took place, as well as Chekhov's former home.

Western Mediterranean

This is a region famous for glamour and holiday fun, combined with all the richness of Spanish, French and Italian culture. At the very western entrance to the Mediterranean is the 18th-century port of **Cádiz**, the nearest port to Seville, with its famous cathedral, bull-ring, Golden Tower and Barrio de Santa Cruz. Not far

MEDITERRANEAN SAFETY TIPS

- **Petty theft** can be a problem in Italian ports. Leave valuables on the ship and keep an eye on your wallet.
- Take care on the **roads** – whether you are travelling by foot, car or moped.
- It is common for tourists to suffer constant – and sometimes aggressive – **hassling** in north African ports. Many visitors find it less tiring to take an organized tour, hire a local guide, or simply stay on the ship!
- Be prepared to encounter overt **prostitution** in some Black Sea ports.
- Genuine **antiques** and religious icons are sometimes sold in Eastern European ports, but following recent crack-downs, such items are likely to be confiscated by government officials.

Western Mediterranean: Don't Miss

Rome (Italy): For first-timers, a sightseeing trip to the Eternal City is a must. See the Vatican, Colosseum, Trevi Fountain, Spanish Steps and St Peter's Square.
French Riviera: Visit the art museums of Nice, enjoy the pretty harbours of St Tropez or Villefranche or take the coastal train to sophisticated Cannes or Monaco.
Florence (Italy): Magnificent Duomo, art galleries, Ponte Vecchio and Pitti Palace.
Pompeii (Italy): Tour the famous archaeological site.
Marrakech (Morocco): Savour the colourful marketplace (Djemma El Fna), characterful streets, water sellers and snake charmers.

away is the equally historic port of **Gibraltar**, the tiny British colony on the tip of Spain. **Málaga** on Spain's southeast coast is principally utilized as an embarkation port, though Picasso's birthplace and museum, the Gibralfaro fortress, or Granada's Alhambra are always worth visiting. North of the beaches of the Costa del Sol is the vibrant city of **Barcelona**, with its famous main street, Las Ramblas, Gaudi's Sagrada Familia cathedral and various art museums.

A large number of cruises take in the **islands** of the western Mediterranean. Palma on **Mallorca**, with its striking cathedral and characterful old town, is an important base port for the region, with the resorts on neighbouring **Menorca** and **Ibiza** always popular. Napoleon's home island, **Corsica**, his first exile residence, **Elba**, and **Sardinia** are all regular ports of call. The style is also turned on along the French coastline at places such as **Marseilles** with its grand old harbour and the enduringly glamorous resorts of the **French Riviera** such as **Nice**, **Villefranche**, **St Tropez**, **Cannes** and **Monte Carlo**.

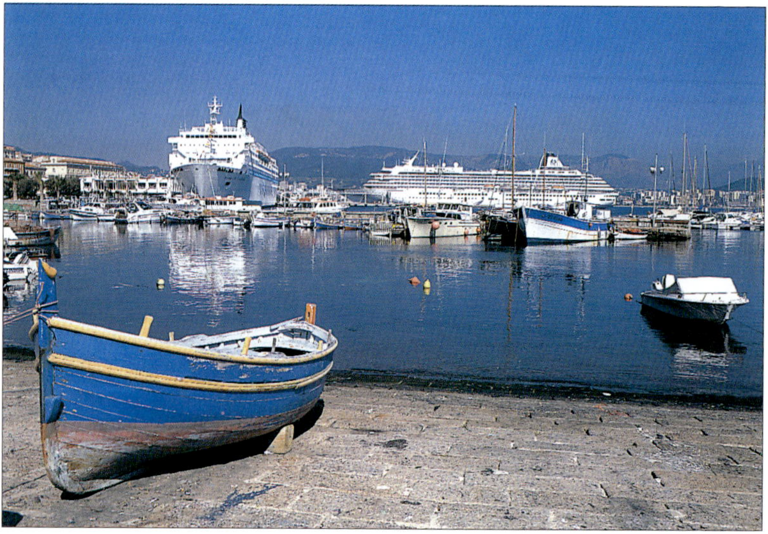

Above: *CUNARD's* Sea Goddess II *in the medieval fortified harbour of Valetta, capital of Malta.*

Opposite: *The contrasts of old and new on the island of Corsica.*

The Italian port of **Genoa**, the birthplace of Columbus, is often used as an embarkation port, although there might be the opportunity to visit the pretty village of **Portofino**. Further along the coast **Livorno** is the gateway to Tuscany, including **Florence** and **Pisa**, while those keen to see **Rome** can get there from the port of **Civitavecchia**. Despite its lovely bay, **Naples** has its share of crime, and many visitors prefer to get out of town to **Pompeii** or to take a hydrofoil over to the island of **Capri**, where a visit to the Blue Grotto makes for a memorable day-trip. Further south the highlights of **Sicily** include the towns of **Taormina** and **Messina**, while **Malta** boasts a spectacular scene as you sail in or out of medieval **Valetta**'s Grand Harbour.

On a cruise in the western Mediterranean you might also get the opportunity of a visit to **north Africa**, visiting places such as **Tunis** in **Tunisia** – the ancient city of Carthage, and Moroccan ports such as white-washed **Tangier**, industrialized **Casablanca**, and **Agadir**, close to the characterful, red-walled **Taroudannt**. Inland are the towns of **Rabat** and **Marrakech**, with its pastel-pink buildings, colourful marketplace and snake charmers.

> **Northern Europe: Don't Miss**
>
> **Amsterdam (The Netherlands)**: Take a canal boat trip, see the Royal Palace, the House of Anne Frank, the Rijksmuseum and the famous red light district.
> **Bergen (Norway)**: Stroll along the wooden-housed waterfront and fish market, see the home of Grieg or take the mountain funicular for superb views.
> **Edinburgh (UK)**: Some magnificent attractions including Edinburgh Castle, the Royal Mile, Holyrood House, the National Gallery of Scotland and Princes Street.
> **London (UK)**: A tourist's paradise. Don't miss Big Ben and the Houses of Parliament, Buckingham Palace, the Tower of London, Trafalgar Square, the West End shows and shopping in Harrod's.
> **Paris (France)**: See the Arc de Triomphe, Eiffel Tower, Champs Elysées, River Seine, Notre Dame Cathedral, Montmartre, Sacré-Coeur Basilica and the Louvre.

Northern Europe

The images of northern Europe are certainly beguiling – the white coast of Greenland, the greenery of Iceland, Scotland's purple highlands, the 'Emerald Isle' of Ireland, the Northern Lights, the Midnight Sun, pubs, castles, fjords. Cooler – and wetter – than the Mediterranean, this region tends to attract mature, destination-minded passengers interested in Europe's rich and varied culture. Passengers are traditionally seasoned travellers in search of a specific experience, as opposed to a last-minute break. Increasingly, however, the combination of breathtaking scenery and exciting city sightseeing is enticing a broader cross-section of visitors

Left: Seabourn Spirit *passes under Tower Bridge as she leaves London.*

and vessels to the region. Alongside the perennial British- and German-marketed fleets, several large US-based lines, including ROYAL CARIBBEAN and COSTA, are now offering regular cruising in northern Europe.

Northern Europe itineraries sometimes reach as far south as **La Coruña** in northern Spain, the chic little resort of **Biarritz** in southern France, and the famous port of **Bordeaux**, a great harbour to enter from the sea and the gateway to some of the world's finest wine-growing areas. In Brittany the popular ports of call include **Brest** and **Saint-Malo**, as well as the **Channel Islands**, although of the five islands only **Jersey** and **Guernsey** can host cruise ships. **Cherbourg** is an attractive town close to the Normandy beaches and cemeteries of the D-Day landings, with the famous tapestry at Bayeaux also well worth a visit.

Rouen is the best port from which to get to **Paris**, while the medieval city of **Ghent** in Belgium, is the access port for equally beautiful **Antwerp**, **Bruges** and **Brussels**. The highlight of the Netherlands is undoubtedly **Amsterdam**, where you can visit diamond-cutting workshops, the Heineken Brewery and the famous red-light district. Along the short North-Sea coast of Germany, **Hamburg** has a colourful port area and can be used to visit the quaint medieval towns of **Mölln**, **Ratzeburg** and **Lübeck**.

NORTHERN EUROPE: WHEN TO GO

Although regional ferries brave these waters year-round, most cruise lines offer only seasonal voyages between **May** and **October**. During this period, average temperatures range from –4°C (25°F) to 12°C (54°F) above the Arctic Circle and from 10°C (50°F) to 28°C (82°F) in northern Spain, with relative variations in between these two extremes. **July and August** are the **warmest** months, but **late June** and **early September** can be good **off-peak** times to explore the region.

Steeped in seafaring tradition, the British Isles are often at their best from the sea. **Dover**'s famous white cliffs make for a fitting gateway, while **Southampton** is a port synonymous with the golden age of great liners. From here you can visit ancient Stonehenge or take a trip to **London** – only small vessels can actually sail under famous Tower Bridge into the centre of the capital.

Visits to Ireland are always popular, with ports-of-call including **Cork**, **Dublin** and **Waterford**, home of the famous crystal glass factory and an annual opera festival (in September). The **Isle of Man** is included in many itineraries, while the array of **Scottish Islands** are a great place for bird-, seal- and other wildlife-spotting. On the east coast of Scotland lies Leith, the port for **Edinburgh**.

The far northwest of Europe has some spectacular scenery, especially during the long summer days when darkness hardly falls. Towns such as **Trondheim** and **Bergen** on the Norwegian coast have pretty wooden houses and engrossing museums, and act as a gateway for the magnificent scenery of the Norwegian Fjords. Even further north is **Tromsø**, where you can see the Northern Lights Planetarium, Tromsdalen Church (the 'Arctic Cathedral') and the Polar Museum, and the **North Cape**, accessible from tiny **Honnigsvaag**. Far into the Greenland Sea is **Spitzbergen**, the name of a glacial archipelago which is Europe's most northerly point of land, while also out in the chilly northern Atlantic are

Right: Hebridean Princess *in tranquil waters off the rugged west coast of Scotland.*

Left: *Geirangerfiord, one of the seemingly endless, breathtaking fjords of Norway's western coastline.*

the rugged **Faroe Islands** and **Iceland**, with its hot springs and geysers, the Golden Waterfall and the old town of **Reykjavik**.

Trips into the **Baltic Sea** are made by a number of cruise lines to explore the intriguing heart of Scandanavia and northeastern Europe. On the way into the Baltic, **Oslo**, the capital of Norway, is one of the world's most charming cities, as is **Copenhagen**, the capital of Denmark. **Stockholm** in Sweden is a clean and cultured city whose highlights include the Royal Palace and Skansen open-air 'living' museum, while **Helsinki** in Finland is a place of pilgrimage for music lovers, who come to see the Sibelius Monument and Finlandia Concert Hall. **St Petersburg** in Russia is a fading jewel of a city, with grand architecture, wistful canals, pot-holed avenues and a magnificent cultural heritage. The winding streets of the medieval walled city of **Tallinn** in Estonia are less well known by tourists, who will also be fascinated by the quaint medieval Old Quarter of **Riga** in Latvia. The German ports of Warnemunde and Travemunde on the Baltic act as access points for the historic city of **Berlin**.

BALTIC SEA: DON'T MISS

Oslo (Norway): See the Hollmenkollen Ski Jump, the Royal Palace and Vigeland's sculptures in Frogner Park.
Copenhagen (Denmark): Stroll through the Tivoli Gardens, shop in Stroget street and visit Christienborg and Amalienborg palaces.
St Petersburg (Russia): Magnificent cultural heritage. Visit the Hermitage art museum, Peter and Paul Fortess, the Summer Palace at Petrodvorets and shop on Nevsky Prospekt.
Stockholm (Sweden): Explore the old town and *bijou* shops, see the Royal Palace, Drottningholm Palace and the restored ancient *Wasa* warship.

> **THE INDIAN OCEAN: DON'T MISS**
>
> **Cape Town (South Africa)**: Take a cable-car up Table Mountain, a coastal drive to the Cape of Good Hope and a wine-tasting tour, and don't miss the view as you sail in or out!
>
> **Mombasa (Kenya)**: Take a safari trip – preferably overnight – to a game park, visit the Arabic-style old town, Fort Jesus and white beaches.
>
> **Mumbai (India):** A fascinating city in a fascinating country, see the famous Gateway of India, the colonial Taj Mahal Hotel, Prince of Wales Museum and Hanging Gardens.
>
> **Zanzibar (Tanzania)**: See the poignant church on the former slave market site, the carved doors of old Stone Town, the former Sultans' Palace, spice bazaar, home of David Livingstone and notorious Prison Island.

THE INDIAN OCEAN

There are four recognized cruising regions around the Indian Ocean: south and west Africa, East Africa and the Seychelles, the Middle East and coastal India. Already of particular appeal to naturalists, scuba divers, and travellers seeking a more unusual cultural experience, cruising here is beginning to attract a much broader market – especially when combined with an African safari or overland visit to a world-famous site such as the Egyptian pyramids or the Taj Mahal.

Cruises down the west coast of Africa are rare, although certain ports, such as **Banjul** in The Gambia and **Dakar** in Senegal, where poignant slavery memorabilia is kept on Goree Island, are sometimes seen on repositioning cruises. The Atlantic islands are also occasional ports-of-call: **São Tiago** on the Cape Verde islands has beautiful beaches and seafood, whereas the rugged British colony of **St Helena** offers a trip back in time,

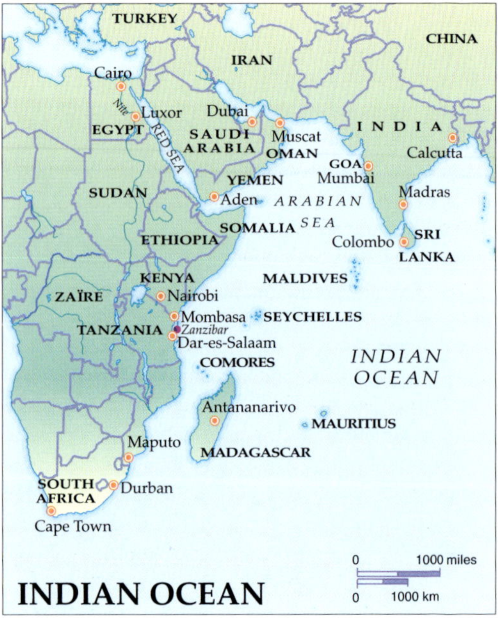

with old fortifications and the house where Napoleon lived while in exile.

Cape Town in South Africa is one of the world's great cruising landmarks, with a host of interesting attractions, while **Durban**, with its fine beaches and nearby wildlife, often acts as a link to the islands of the western part of the Indian Ocean, including beautiful **Mauritius**, volcanic **Réunion Island** and fascinating **Madagascar**. Between Madagascar and the African mainland are the **Comores** islands, while on the East African coast the main ports are **Zanzibar**, the exotic former sultanate, and **Mombasa** in Kenya, a great place to take a safari trip. A popular destination for up-market cruising is the **Seychelles** group, lying off East Africa, which include **Mahé**, **Praslin**, and **La Digue**, a charming island to be explored by foot, bicycle or ox-cart.

Above: The Marco Polo *cruising in one of the many jewels of the Indian Ocean, the Seychelles.*

Many cruises in the Middle East and Red Sea areas begin at **Port Suez** in Egypt, the gateway to the Suez Canal and overland visits to Luxor and Cairo. Other Egyptian ports along the Red Sea are **Safaga**, a great spot for diving, and **Sharm el Sheik**, from where you can take a 4- wheel-drive tour into the Sinai Desert. Further down the Red Sea, the ports of **Al Hudaydah** and **Aden** in Yemen offer the chance to see some fascinating architecture.

In the Arabian Sea, the town of **Muscat** in Oman is a fascinating walled city with Portuguese influences, while modern **Dubai** in the United Arab Emirates is the place

Right: *The Swedish-built* Andaman Princess, *owned by* SIAM CRUISE, *offers reasonably priced cruises in the Andaman Sea and the Gulf of Thailand.*

to take a traditional dhow boat trip, bargain for gold in the souks or bet on camels at the race track. You can also take a dhow trip at **Al Manamah** on Bahrain, the 'island of a million palms', as well as scuba dive or shop for pearls and handicrafts.

One of the true highlights of India, **Mumbai** (until recently known as Bombay) batters the senses. Here you can enjoy the famous Gateway of India, Victorian architecture, characterful open-air laundries, Chowpatty Beach and Elephanta Caves. **Mormugao** reveals Goa's Portuguese-Indian blend of styles, beautiful beaches and tourist resorts, while **New Mangalore** offers a glimpse of urban India and its ubiquitous contrasts. **Madras** is another city of dramatic cultural contrasts, with colonial architecture, a characterful city and white beaches, as is **Calcutta**, a place of dire poverty, bustling streets, colonial buildings and famous temples. Off the coast of India, the island of **Sri Lanka** has a rich culture and many attractive resorts, whereas exotic **Malé** in the **Maldives** is a place to see rare birds, giant turtles, blue seas and palm-fringed beaches in a divers' and snorkellers' paradise.

THE INDIAN OCEAN: WHEN TO GO

With the notable year-round exception of AFRICAN SAFARI CLUB's *Royal Star* and several cargo-passenger lines (*see* Chapter 7), most cruise ships sail these waters between **November** and **April**, when general humidity is at its lowest. During these months, average temperatures range between 12°C (54°F) and 33°C (91°F), but tropical rains should be expected, especially in the **Seychelles** and **Madagascar** (these particular islands are actually better visited between **June** and **September**).

Southeast Asia and the Far East

This is a region which looks set to receive a huge increase in cruise tourism – not only in the shape of westerners coming to discover the mysteries of the East, but also from its own burgeoning domestic market. Japan has always had a strong cruise tradition through companies such as NYK and Mitsui OSK, but now a new breed of Southeast Asian passenger is being drawn by Singapore's Star Cruise and Metro Holdings, Indonesia's Spice Island Cruises and Awani Cruises and Thailand's Siam Cruise.

On the northern fringe of the core cruising area of Southeast Asia is **Yangon** in Myanmar, the city formerly known as Rangoon and home to the colonial Strand Hotel and the magnificent Shwe Dagon Pagoda. Moving south, the stretch of Thailand's coast on the Indian Ocean includes **Phuket**, with its lively beaches, bars and hotels, with the Malaysian island of **Langkawi** and the port of **Penang** located by the edge of the famous Straits of Malacca. Also here is **Port Kelang**, the gateway to **Kuala Lumpur**, while at the tip of the Malaysian peninusla is

SE Asia and The Far East: When To Go

The cruising season here runs primarily between **October** and **March**. This is not, however, a guarantee of optimum weather. **Indonesia** is prone to **monsoons** during these months and winter temperatures in **Beijing** can reach as low as –8°C (17°F). Seasonal temperatures vary enormously from region to region, and tropical rains and humidity are prevalent. Nevertheless, **February** and **October** are arguably the most temperate months to visit **Singapore**, **January** and **February** for **Myanmar**, **April** and **May** for **Korea** and **Japan**, and **November** to **February** for **Thailand**.

SE Asia and The Far East: Don't Miss

Bali (Indonesia): Enjoy Kuta Beach, the Barong Dance, Balinese temples, artists' villages and barter for wood carvings and batik fabrics.
Ho Chi Minh City (Vietnam): See the Reunification Palace, war museums, Notre Dame Cathedral or head for fascinating underground Cu Chi.
Hong Kong: Discover malls, floating restaurants, characterful alleys, Nathan Road, the view from Victoria Peak, and take a sampan past the houseboats of Aberdeen or a hydrofoil to Macau.
Singapore: Take a trishaw through Chinatown or a cable-car to magical Sentosa Island, then finish off with a Singapore Sling in the Long Bar of Raffles Hotel.
Beijing (China): See Tiananmen Square, the Forbidden City, Temple of Heaven, Summer Palace and, time permitting, the Great Wall and Ming Tombs.

Opposite: *Swan Hellenic's* Minerva *alongside in Ho Chi Minh City, Vietnam.*

Singapore, the city-state with an incredible blend of oriental, colonial and ultra-modern.

On the other side of the Straits of Malacca is the Indonesian island of **Sumatra**, with the rest of the archipelago of Indonesia spreading out to the east. On **Java**, the port capital of **Jakarta** is an urban mass of contrasts, while **Semarang** provides the cruise ship gateway to the magnificent temple of Borobudur. **Bali** has some splendid resort hotels, lush greenery, temples and artists' villages, and neighbouring **Lombok** presents a quieter version of Bali. On the island of **Komodo**, a lush national park, you are escorted on foot by rangers to view the huge lizards known as Komodo Dragons, while there are also unusual sights on the large volcanic island of **Sulawesi** with the Torajan gravesites and their strange effigies. There are some 17,000 islands scattered betwen Sumatra and Borneo, collectively known as the **Spice Islands**. Look out for unusual plant-life on volcanic **Flores**, mountain villages and buffalo races on **Sumbawa**, 'dancing' horse riders on **Lesser Sunda**, and old Portuguese and Dutch influences on **Timor**.

The islands of the **Philippines** also offer some diverse attractions, including **Manila**, a crowded capital of colourful contrasts, **Mindanao Island**, with tropical parklands and fine beaches, and the **Visayan Islands**, including Cebu's Fort San Pedro and Magellan's Cross, wonderful beaches and the Chocolate Hills of neighbouring Bohol.

Returning to the mainland, **Laem Chabang** in Thailand is the port for **Bangkok** and its wats (temples), klongs (canals), micro-dressed bar girls and saffron-robed monks. Vietnam has a number of fascinating ports, including **Ho Chi Minh City**, formerly Saigon, **Nha Trang**, with lovely beaches, colourful market scenes and historic ruins, **Da Nang**, beside the famous China Beach, and **Haiphong**, the cruise port for **Hanoi**. Off the south coast of China lies tropical **Hainan**, while a little further east are the dynamic cities of **Guangzhou** (Canton) and **Hong Kong**, the famous harbour of skyscrapers, ferry boats and junks. **Shanghai** is China's

main port, with the capital, **Beijing**, served by the ports of **Tianjin** and **Xingang**. **Seoul**, the capital of South Korea, is served by **Inchon**, though an equally fascinating port to visit in this country is **Pusan**, where you can see the huge Chagalchi fish market, Pomosa Buddhist Temple and United Nations Cemetery.

Across the Korean Strait from here lies Japan, an increasingly important cruise destination. At **Nagasaki** you can see the poignant museum of the atomic bomb drop in the International Cultural Hall, the pretty Peace Park and Glover House of Madame Butterfly fame; further round the coast lies **Kagoshima** and the pretty spa resort of Ibusuki, while **Kobe**, largely rebuilt after the 1995 earthquake, is only a 'bullet train' ride from historic **Kyoto**, with its Sanjusangendo Temple, ornate buildings and pink cherry trees. Kyoto can also be visited from **Osaka**, home of Japan's largest castle, the stone lanterns of Sumiyoshi Shrine and the festive boats of Temmangu Shrine. **Yokohama** is the port for **Tokyo** and the place from which to visit the lovely Fuji-Hakone-Izu National Park or the famous bronze Buddha at Kamakura.

SE ASIA: STAYING SAFE

- The law in many Southeast Asian countries is harsh on offenders of **drug**-related crimes. Avoid illegal drugs and beware of accepting unfamiliar parcels.
- In **Singapore**, don't litter or smoke in public places, eat or drink on the subway, jay-walk on the roadway, or even chew gum!
- Many sex-related shows and services in **Thailand** involve the exploitation of minors. To patronize them encourages this malpractice.
- Expect to be plagued by persistent **hawkers** in tourist areas throughout Indonesia. Show even a flicker of interest and you are destined to return home with umpteen sarongs, tropical fish mobiles, batik shirts, wicker baskets and wooden banana trees!

The South Pacific

The South Pacific is a region able to stir up endless evocative images: grass skirts, gently swaying *tamure* dancers, Paul Gauguin paintings, coral reefs, tropical flora, volcanic peaks, talcum white beaches and blue, blue waters. Australasia is also a place with impressive, though less tropical, scenery, combined with a sporty, laid-back culture and its own indigenous heritage. Souvenir hunters will enjoy looking for Aboriginal and Maori arts and crafts; sports fans will appreciate the many surfing, diving and outdoor recreational options; and culture buffs and naturalists will be attracted by the region's clean cities, fine museums and excellent nature reserves.

In the light of all this, it is perhaps surprising that few mainstream cruise ships currently venture 'down under'.

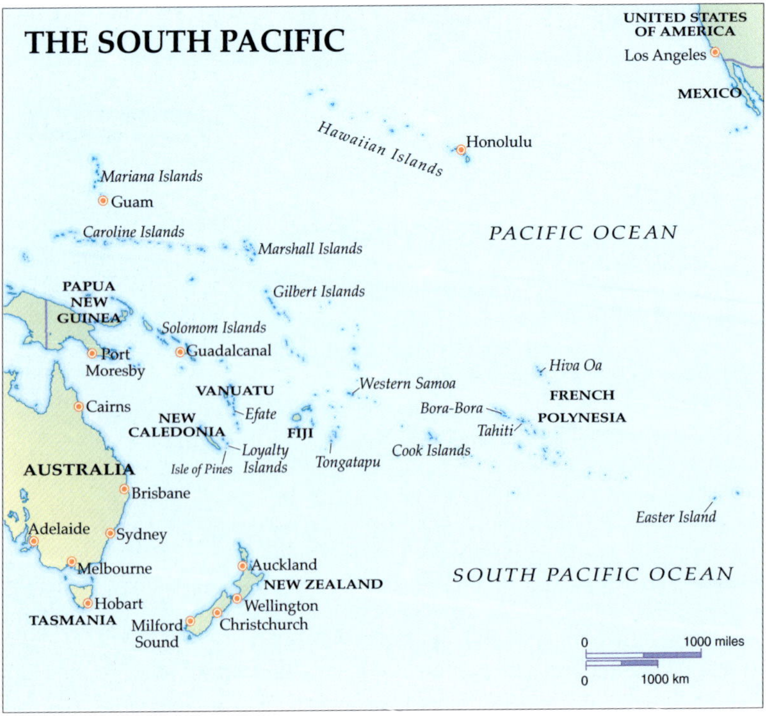

Above: *Half a cruise ship, half a sailing yacht:* Windsong *from the unique* WINDSTAR *fleet is anchored here in Bora Bora.*

The region's distance from the main American and European cruise markets is an obvious factor. But as the giant lines seek new playgrounds and the industry opens up to include the vast Southeast Asian marketplace, so Oceania (the name often given to the huge sweep of South Pacific islands) and Australasia could find themselves opening up rapidly to cruising.

Long associated with WINDSTAR (although *Wind Song* has now been repositioned to Costa Rica), Tahiti has been selected as the base port for RADISSON SEVEN SEAS' appropriately named *Paul Gauguin*. MARINE EXPEDITIONS offers off-beat South Pacific itineraries and AMERICAN HAWAII CRUISES sails year-round between the islands of the eponymous US state. The ships of ORIENT, P&O, HAPAG-LLOYD and PRINCESS CRUISES, together with regional coastal cruisers, sailing vessels and passenger-cargo ships regularly sail these waters and vessels undertaking world cruises or global itineraries may also call at selected ports throughout the region.

Probably the most exotic of the South Pacific islands are those of **French Polynesia**, most famously **Tahiti**, though quickly followed by beautiful **Moorea**, **Raiatea**

THE SOUTH PACIFIC: WHEN TO GO

Most cruise ships sail these waters between **November** and **April**. This, however, coincides with high humidity and tropical rains in Oceania and Australasia's hottest season. Arguably the best months are **May** and **September**, when humidity is lower and peak temperatures average 32°F (90°) in French Polynesia, 19°C (66°F) in Sydney and 28°C (82°F) in Cairns. **Tasmania** and **New Zealand** are milder than mainland Australia.

THE SOUTH PACIFIC: DON'T MISS

Auckland (New Zealand): See Maori artifacts, shop at Victoria Park Market, do a bungee jump, visit the Underwater World Aquarium and the bubbling mud and geysers of Rotorua.
Bora Bora (French Polynesia): Explore this coral-fringed paradise by foot, bicycle or moped and don't miss the island view as you sail in and out.
Milford Sound (New Zealand): Enjoy spectacular views as your ship explores this famous fjord.
Oahu (Hawaii): From Honolulu, visit Waikiki beach, Polynesian Cultural Center, Punchbowl Crater and Cemetery and poignant Pearl Harbour.
Sydney (Australia): Don't miss the superb view of the Opera House 'sails', the 'Coathanger' bridge and the city skyline as you sail in.

and coral-fringed **Bora Bora**. On the distant Marquesas group of islands, the highlight is **Hiva Oa**, the island where Paul Gauguin lived and died, while even more remote is **Easter Island**, territory owned by Chile, home of the strange head-shaped monoliths.

On the island of **Viti Levu** in the **Fiji** group you can still see evidence of cannibalism in Suva's Fiji Museum, as well as dancers and fire-walkers at the Fijian Cultural Center. **Apia** in **Western Samoa** has the home and mountain grave of Robert Louis Stevenson, while **Pago Pago** in **American Samoa** is another small, colourful, welcoming town. On **Tongatapu** in the **Tonga** group look out for the Royal Palace and the Chapel and Tombs, as well as simply strolling around lush tropical gardens and buying *tapa* (bark cloth) handicrafts at **Nuku'Alofa**'s bustling market.

Efate in the Vanuatu group is a place for reef adventures, game fishing or shopping, while the **New Caledonia Islands** boast a chic capital, **Noumea**, beautiful beaches, the lush scenery of the **Loyalty Islands** and the tall trees unique to lovely **Isle of Pines**. Other places to visit in this eastern part of Oceania include **Port Moresby** on Papua New Guinea, **Guadalcanal** in the Solomon Islands, and **Guam**, one of the Mariana Islands, a tropical base for the US military and Japanese tourists, and location of the Blue Hole, a famous dive site.

The **Hawaiian** islands are commonly included within South Pacific itineraries. On **Maui**, you can spot whales, visit sugar plantations, or take a submarine trip, on **Oahu** is Honolulu, Waikiki beach and the Arizona Memorial at Pearl Harbour, while on **Kaui** the attractions include Waimea Canyon, Koloa, Princeville the view from Ne Pali.

The cities of **Australia** are well-endowed with attractions: largest and most spectacular is **Sydney**, one of the world's great harbours; **Brisbane** has koalas and kangaroos at the Lone Pine Sanctuary and surfing on the Gold Coast; **Cairns** is the port for the magnificent Great Barrier Reef; while a stop in **Darwin** allows you to head for the outback and spectacular Kakadu National Park. **Fremantle** is the charming Victorian port for **Perth**, **Adelaide** is an attractive, spacious town in the heart of the wine-making Barossa Valley, and from **Melbourne** you can head to the Dandenong Ranges and Healesville Sanctuary. **Hobart** is the picturesque capital of Tasmania, and from **Devonport** you can visit the island's Cradle Mountain and Lake St Clair National Park.

New Zealand may be more remote and much smaller, but it is still a country packed with things to do or see. Its main city, **Auckland**, is another of the world's most dramatic cruise ports. North of the city, the **Bay of Islands** is a place for deep-sea fishing and wildlife-spotting, while at the south of North island is the capital, **Wellington**, with magnificent harbour views from the top of Mt Victoria. On the South Island are the contrasts of civilized **Christchurch** with the magnificent coastal scenery of the **Marlborough Sounds** and the spectacular **Milford Sound** fjord.

Above: *Sydney Harbour, one of the world's classic cruise destinations.*
Opposite: *Snorkelling off the back of an explorer craft on Australia's Great Barrier Reef.*

THE SOUTH PACIFIC: TRAVEL TIPS

- The islands of the South Pacific can be extremely hot and humid. Wear cool **loose-fitting clothes** and try to avoid mid-day sightseeing.
- **French Polynesia** is not cheap. If your priority is shopping or eating out, put aside some serious spending money.
- Unlike most ports of this region, **Port Moresby** in Papua New Guinea has a very high crime rate. Avoid venturing off alone (especially to Paga Hill or Hanauabada) and leave valuables on the ship.

7
Alternative Cruising

Diverging from its conventional image, cruising also embraces the more unusual holiday experience, taking you off the beaten track in a variety of different and interesting ways. Wind-powered vessels, such as tall sail ships, are enjoying a revival and a number of cargo ships also carry passengers across the globe. For the adventurous, explorer vessels set off to the Antarctic or other intriguing regions, while those seeking a more relaxed means of discovering a specific region might take a traditional riverboat.

LUXURY CARGO

Don't be misled into thinking that cargo ships are smelly, rusting hulks – IVARAN LINES' *Americana*, for example, is an exceptionally well-appointed cargo vessel, carrying up to 88 passengers in *en suite* accommodations with TV, video, mini bar, refrigerator, telephone and personal safe. It boasts a lounge with dance floor, bars, casino, library, hairdresser, sauna/jacuzzi, health club, swimming pool and hospital.

CARGO SHIPS

A number of cargo ships (sometimes called freighters) carry passengers in addition to their regular crew and cargo. Such ships fall into several categories – **container ships**, which carry an assortment of goods packed into large standardized metal cases (containers); **refrigerated ships**, which transport fresh produce in refrigerated compartments; **bulk carriers**, which house non-packaged freight such as coal, grain or liquids; **roll-on roll-off** (ro-ro) ships, widely used for ferrying vehicles; **tramp steamers**, which follow irregular and unpredictable itineraries; and **passenger-cargo ships**, a compromise between freighters and regular cruise ships which carry at least 12 (and maybe more than 100) passengers. For potential passengers, each of these categories offers something different – container ships, for example, usually provide the most reliable service, whereas bulk carriers allow passengers more time in port (bulk takes

Opposite: *The billowing sails of one of the cruising world's most impressive large sailing yachts, the* Søren Larsen.

longer to off-load); refrigerated ships tend to sail faster while tramp steamers have a romantic air of adventure and unpredictability and passenger cargo ships have more amenities on offer to their guests.

Life Aboard a Cargo Ship

Cargo ships can carry a huge miscellany of freight, from machinery parts to sunflower seeds. However, any transporting **dangerous freight** (such as petroleum or chemical products) are not allowed to carry passengers. For passengers, a well laden ship can mean a **smoother** ride, as a cargo ship will generally sit lower in the water than a cruise ship, and it will also quite often mean a slower (and therefore more relaxed) journey. However, the nature of the freight commonly means that cargo ships are given poorer **docking allocations** than cruise ships – this can be a disadvantage if port facilities are further away and taxis less easily available, although it will mean you are less likely to be targeted by the bands of hawkers often found by cruise ship berths.

A significant difference between the life of a cruise ship passenger and that of one on a cargo ship is that freighters do not tend to offer **organized activities** or **shore excursions**.

While this obviously attracts the independent traveller happy to entertain themselves, most cargo ships have more amenities than many people realise – a comfortable lounge, dining room, bar, laundry facilities, deckspace for walking or sunbathing, and maybe a small pool, video lounge, sauna, gymnasium or library. In fact, levels of service tend to be high on cargo ships; while pampering is not on the agenda, basic services are han-

MEDICAL COVER

Cargo ships carrying 12 passengers or less are not legally obliged to carry a ship's doctor, and emergency cases may have to be evacuated to a nearby vessel or shoreside hospital. It is particularly important to take out a **travel health insurance policy** (including evacuation cover) when undertaking a voyage of this type. Potential cargo-ship passengers should also be aware that:

- Many ships impose an **upper age limit** (usually 75 or 80) and passengers may have to provide medical proof that they are fit to travel. Some lines also have a **minimum** age for travel.
- Most vessels insist that passengers must be able to climb stairwell ladders and walk unassisted. Cargo ships are not suitable for wheelchairs, walking frames and sticks.

dled by a small team of stewards who often double as cabin-cleaners and waiters. The standard of accommodation is often high, with well-sized cabins, and dining, usually taken in the officers' dining room, can be of a good quality. The low passenger carry and the fact that officers, passengers and crew mix together at meals and other times means that cargo ships offer a **congenial atmosphere**. It is worth noting, however, that unlike regular cruise ships, meal hours are scheduled around the workings of the crew.

Booking A Cargo-Ship Voyage

Before booking a trip on a cargo ship, it is important to be aware of certain aspects of their routine. Because these are 'working' ships and their priority is the delivery of the freight rather than the convenience of the passenger, cargo ships do not always run to schedule. However, the nature of the business of cargo ships also means that they sail all over the globe, giving you a wide choice of destination and itinerary.

Contrary to general opinion, cargo ships are not necessarily a cheaper option. Prices for cargo ship holidays are comparable to the lower prices of mid-range conventional cruise ships. On the other hand, good deals do exist and one of the largest passenger-carrying cargo lines, Polish Ocean Lines, offers particularly competitive rates.

Cargo Ship Information

The following agencies specialize in providing relevant information and booking freighter travel:

In the United Kingdom: Cargo Ship Voyages, Gdynia America Lines, Gill's Travel and Strand Voyages. The latter also publishes a colour brochure, covering over 30 shipping lines.

In the United States: Anytime Anywhere Travel, CDP Travel, Freighter World Cruises Inc. (which also publishes the fortnightly *Freighter Space Advisory*), Pearl's Travel Tips, Sea The Difference Inc. and Travltips (which also publishes *Roam the World by Freighter* and a bi-monthly members' magazine).

In Canada: Freighter Cruise Service, Hagen's Travel and The Cruise People.

In Germany: Frachtschiff-Touristik, Hamburg Süd and Hamburger Abendblatt/Die Welt.

In Switzerland: Wagner Frachtschiffreisen.

In France: Mer et Voyages and Le Cargo Club. The latter is not an agency but a French meeting place, bookshop and information exchange on freighter travel.

Opposite: *The* Contship New Zealand, *a fully fledged cargo ship which can accommodate paying passengers, and* (**Left**) *the* RMS St Helena, *a multi-purpose passenger-cargo vessel with room for over 100 passengers.*

Other Sailing Ship Operators

AB Sea Cruises/Sailing School in Australia offers sail training and yacht racing adventures aboard *Red Rizla*.
Captain Cook Cruises operates the tall ships *Ra Marama* and *Rubaiyyat* out of Fiji.
Clyde Offshore Sailing Centre in Scotland offers long-distance sail voyages, including a 15-month round-the-world voyage.
Greek Islands Cruise Center markets 20-passenger sailing yachts for Aegean island-hopping.
Leisure Cruises of Switzerland offers Turkish coastal cruises aboard the tall ship *Druzhba*.
Metropolitan Touring markets the Galápagos itineraries of the brigantine *Diamant* and ketch *Rachel III*.
Nautical Resources, Inc. is a yacht charter firm with a fine trio of sailing ships, the *Colombaio Sky*, *Star* and *Sun*.
Songlines Cruises operates the deluxe sailboat *Maruta Wind* throughout Indonesia.
Traverse Tall Ship Company operates topsail schooner *Manitou* on Lakes Michigan and Huron.
Vermont Schooner Cruises sails the schooner *Homer W. Dixon* on Lake Champlain.
Wilderness Travel markets the off-beat Galápagos itineraries of brigantine schooner, *Andando* and twin-masted yacht, *La Violante*, out of Fiji.
Worldwide Adventures offers tall ship voyages around the Greek Islands, Oceania and the Maldives.
Worldwide Travel & Cruise Associates markets several vessels with global itineraries.

Sailing Ships and Yachts

For romantics and adventurers, a cruise on board a sailing ship offers a nostalgic and tranquil passage through some of the world's most beautiful waters and, even if you are not inclined to scale the rigging or take a turn at the helm, a sailing ship or yacht can still provide a delightfully different type of holiday.

Cruising on a sailing ship, however, is noticeably different to conventional cruising. Sailing cruises tend to follow **more unusual itineraries** than conventional cruise ships, and are more likely to change route, depending on the weather. They rarely provide **organized activities** or **entertainment** and most (with the exception of Windstar ships) do not have a casino, putting their emphasis more on offering an **adventurous** style of cruise – with watersports a particular favourite.

Their passenger carry is often very low, making the atmosphere on board **relaxed** and **friendly** (you will be expected to be sociable). **Dress** is informal and **dining** is generally open sitting with the emphasis on good simple cooking rather than real gourmet cuisine. Beach and deck barbecues are a popular feature. You are also likely to have more **personal contact** with the officers and crew than on conventional cruise ships and, at the officers' discretion, you may be able to take an active part in sailing the ship.

The main disadvantages of this style of cruising are that you are more likely to feel the motion of the sea, and that sailing ships are generally unsuitable for **young children** or those with **mobility problems** (a notable exception to this being the specially equipped *SS Lord Nelson* – *see* Chapter 4).

The principal companies offering sailing cruises are as follows:

Compagnie des Isles du Ponant

Competing in the hi-tech, luxury sail-cruiser market is the small (1500grt) *Le Ponant*, owned by the Nantes-based Compagnie des Isles du Ponant. Sailing out of Guadeloupe for winter Caribbean cruises and

Above: *The informal life of a sailing cruise.*

Marseilles during its Mediterranean summer, this sleek vessel provides a very chic experience for up to 60 passengers.

Like the ships of Windstar, *Le Ponant* features computerized sails, elegant interiors and a stern platform for its extensive watersports programme. It also provides more deck space than Windstar's ships and has an equally shallow draft, allowing access to less frequented ports. A distinctly continental ambience prevails with French officers and crew, and youthful, sophisticated guests who appreciate good food, good wine and good (French-speaking) company.

Deilmann Reedererei (Peter Deilmann River & Ocean Cruises)

The recently built (1994) *Lili Marleen* is a classic three-masted barquentine, the dream of owner Peter Deilmann, who markets his creation to a maximum of 50 passengers per cruise – mostly Germans who appreciate the familiar ambience afforded by German-speaking officers and staff and good quality German-style cooking. Unlike the hi-tech sail-cruisers that rely on engine propulsion as much as wind power, *Lili Marleen* only occasionally reverts to her engines.

Dirigo Cruises

This US-based company markets an extensive choice of tall ships and other sailing vessels on varied itineraries that include coastal USA, the Caribbean and the South Pacific. Of particular interest not only to sailors but also to scuba divers and naturalists are what Dirigo themselves describe as 'the world's largest and most luxurious

Nautical Terms

The names and descriptions used for sailing ships and yachts can seem bewildering, although in fact the terms used are designed to be quite accurate:

- A **yacht** tends to be a smaller and lighter sailing boat. Yachts with only one mast are referred to as sloops.
- A **schooner** can describe any size of vessel with two masts of approximately equal height.
- A **brigantine** is a two-masted vessel with a square-rigged foremast.
- A **barque**, **bark** or **barquentine** has three masts, with at least one of these square-rigged.
- A **catamaran** has two hulls, as opposed to the conventional one, while a **trimaran** has three hulls.

WINDJAMMIN' EVENTS

Throughout the summer months, various windjammer events are held in Maine. Boothay hosts the **Windjammer Days Sailing Parade** on the last Wednesday in June; the **Great Schooner Race** takes place between North Haven and Rockland Breakwater during the Fourth of July week; and *WoodenBoat* magazine hosts a windjammer **get-together** at Eggemoggin Reach in the second week in September. For passengers on board Maine Windjammer Association vessels who are in the right place at the right time, these colourful events can be a highlight of their time aboard.

trimarans', *Cuan Law* and *Lammer Law*. Accommodating 18 passengers apiece, these unusual vessels offer year-round cruising around the Caribbean (out of Tortola) and the Galápagos Islands (out of San Cristobal).

Galileo Cruises

The *Galileo* is a classic twin-masted motor-cruiser accommodating up to 40 passengers. She spends summers in the Mediterranean and winters touring the beautiful islands of the Seychelles. Windsurfing, snorkelling and fishing equipment is kept on board, although the emphasis remains firmly on the setting rather than activities.

Maine Windjammer Association

The northeastern USA is a justifiably popular sailing region, and this association represents many of the fine traditional ships in these waters. These include the *Angelique*, *J & E Riggin*, *Lewis R French*, *Grace Bailey*, *Mary Day*, *Nathaniel Bowditch*, *Roseway*, *Shenandoah* and the largest US-registered windjammer, *Victoria Chimes*.

The accommodation on most Maine Windjammer ships is basic but comfortable, the food hearty (with lobster bakes a popular feature) and entertainment is limited to the sailing adventures of the ship itself. The season runs from June to September, with cruises generally lasting between three and seven days.

North End Shipyard Schooners

Also represented by the Maine Windjammer Association are the lovely sailing ships of North End Shipyard Schooners. The oldest of the fleet of three, *Isaac H Evans*, was built in 1886 and has been fully restored to carry 20 passengers; *American Eagle*, launched in 1930, was part of Gloucester's fishing fleet for more than half a century before being refurbished to carry 28 passengers; and the 33-passenger *Heritage* was built in 1983 to combine tradition with modern comfort. The only group of Maine Windjammers to specialize in family vacations, two of the trio (*American Eagle* and *Isaac H Evans*) have been designated National Historic Landmarks.

Sea Cloud Cruises

Tall ship enthusiasts will admire the magnificent *Sea Cloud* – the 30-sail barquentine currently gracing the waters of the Mediterranean and Caribbean. Built in Germany in 1931 for Marjorie Merrieweather Post by her financier husband, E. F. Hutton, the vessel was, at the time, the largest private yacht ever launched. It has since carried numerous celebrities and was even used as a naval weather station during World War II. *Sea Cloud* is now owned by a German consortium and frequently sails under charter.

Lovingly restored to include wood panelling and antique furnishings along the lines of the original interiors, this is arguably the most luxurious – and expensive – ship of its type. In spite of its price tag, however, the dress code is casual and the atmosphere relaxed. There is also a distinctly European ambience (including German officers and crew members) which appeals to its predominantly European passengers.

All At Sea

In addition to *Sea Cloud*, the booking company **Ocean Voyages** can organize sailing trips on:

- The *Tequila*, a 14m (46ft) racing sloop that explores the natural beauty of New Zealand's Bay of Islands.
- The *Infinity*, also a 14m racing sloop, based in the Grenadines and offering wonderful snorkelling in the Tobago Cays.
- Several 6-passenger yachts that follow the nature trail in Sweden's scenic Stockholm Archipelago.
- The square-rigged, 16-passenger ship, *Eye of the Wind*, originally launched in 1911 and now offering excellent diving opportunities in the Vanuatu and Solomon Islands, Papua New Guinea and the Great Barrier Reef off Australia's northeast coast.
- The *Archipels*, a 17m (57ft) catamaran which island hops between Huahine and Bora Bora in French Polynesia.
- The motor yacht *Midnight Sun*, which explores parts of the Alaskan coastline which are inaccessible to mainstream cruise ships.
- The *Sea Maiden*, a classic sailing yacht offering 7-day wildlife-spotting trips in the USA's Channel Islands National Park.
- Several yachts that explore the 'real' Hawaii – the bays and reefs of Lanai, Maui, Molokai and Oahu that tourists rarely discover.

Left: *The majestic* Sea Cloud *alongside at St John's in Antigua.*

SAILING STARS

The dream of Swedish yachtsman, Mikael Krafft, was realized when he commissioned the Belgian dockyard, Scheepswerven van Langerbrugge, to construct two authentic barquentine schooners for his White Star Group (the Belgian parent company of Star Clippers). The tallest ships in the world when they were launched in the early 1990s, they are currently the only ships of this type to be fully certified by the US Coastguard and to carry the highest rating of Lloyd's Register of Shipping. *Star Flyer* also has the claim to fame of being the first commercial sailing ship to cross the North Atlantic since the turn of the twentieth century. On occasions when scheduling allows these two schooners to meet, passengers are treated to a unique and spectacular race across the waves.

Square Sail Pacific

Fans of the British television series *The Onedin Line* will be familiar with the billowing outline of the *Søren Larsen*, the star of this and many other film and television productions, including the film *The French Lieutenant's Woman*. The last vessel to be built at the Danish shipyard of Søren Larsen & Sons, the *Søren Larsen* was launched in 1949 and worked as a cargo ship throughout northern Europe until 1972. Saved from the scrapyard and then restored by its dedicated owner and captain, Tony Davies, and his family, this square-masted brigantine is now based in Pacific waters, heading down to New Zealand in the austral summer. A real sailor's ship with creaking timbers and the smell of tallow and tar, the *Søren Larsen* offers a hands-on voyage for up to 22 passengers.

Star Clippers

The tallest sail ships ever to be built, *Star Flyer* and *Star Clipper* were launched in 1991 and 1992 respectively. They each have four masts and sixteen manually furled sails (no automation here!) but bend to modern advances with such features as an anti-rolling system to improve stability. Each ship accommodates up to 180 passengers, typically a cosmopolitan cross-section reflected in the officers and crew, who themselves number around 70. Commanding mid-range sail-ship prices for unusual itineraries in the Caribbean, Mediterranean and the Far East, these ships merge authentic design and traditional decor with ultra-modern conveniences such as well-equipped cabins, swimming pools and a piano bar. As with most real sailing ships,

the ambience is relaxed, the dress code casual and the entertainment suitably low key, with the emphasis on nautical themes. Extensive watersports include scuba diving, windsurfing, water-skiing and snorkelling.

THE GREAT BARRIER REEF

- The Great Barrier Reef is the largest coral reef in the world, and is home to the largest number of marine life forms in the world, including over 1500 species of fish.
- The reef consists of nearly 1000 islands and 3000 individual reefs.
- The total area of the reef is some 350,000km^2 (220,000 square miles).
- Among the larger animals found on the reef are the endangered dugong, and green and loggerhead turtles.

Tall Ship Adventures

Somewhere between a Star Clippers' cruise and a basic windjammer vacation lies the equally hands-on experience of a voyage aboard the *Sir Francis Drake*. Originally launched in 1917, she worked as a trading ship carrying copper from Chile to Europe for many years before being restored in the late 1980s. Her passenger carry (30) is low, which affords a casual, intimate atmosphere sailing the idyllic waters of the Caribbean.

Whitsunday Adventure Sailing

Sailing out of Airlie Beach within easy reach of Australia's Great Barrier Reef, these vessels offer a truly barefoot, hands-on sailing experience combined with unspoiled islands and fabulous underwater scenery. *Coral Trekker*, originally built in Norway in 1939, is a handsome top-sail ketch with distinctive ruby sails; *Windjammer* is a classic gaff-rigged schooner, Australian-built and launched in 1994; and in a completely different vein, *Apollo III* is a sleek ocean racing yacht which was once used as an America's Cup training vessel. The three vessels provide a great outdoors experience – snorkelling, diving, windsurfing, learning the ropes, throwing prawns on the barbecue and even sleeping under star-filled skies on deck, weather permitting.

Opposite: Star Flyer *and* Star Clipper.
Below: *WHITSUNDAY ADVENTURE*'s Coral Trekker *sailing the waters of the Coral Sea.*

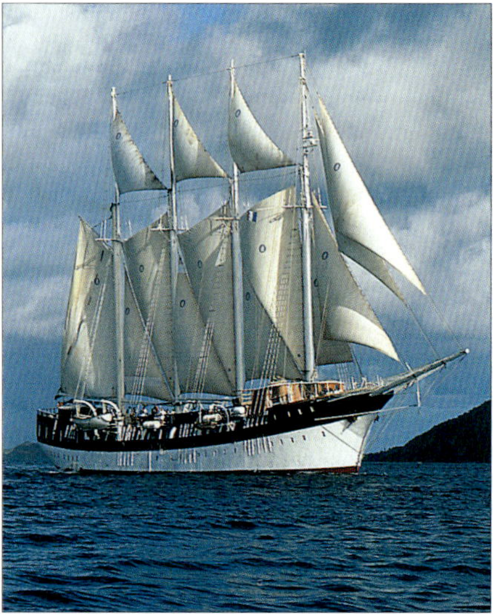

Above: *The* WINDJAMMER *flagship* Fantome.

Windjammer Barefoot Cruises

Visiting some of the less known – and less spoiled – islands of the Caribbean, the beautifully refurbished fleet of tall ship enthusiast Mike Burke offers relatively inexpensive and relaxed cruising. The flagship is the *Fantome* – one of the largest four-masted ships in the world and previously owned by the former Duke of Westminster, the Guinness family and Aristotle Onassis (who intended – but never delivered – her as a wedding gift for Prince Rainier and Princess Grace of Monaco). The three-masted *Mandalay* was built in 1923 and later used as an oceanographic research ship; the *Yankee Clipper* was built in 1927 as an armour-plated yacht for German industrialist Alfred Krupp; the beautiful barquentine *Flying Cloud* was once a French navy training ship; and the *Polynesia* – an extensively refurbished fishing schooner – is noted for its regular singles' cruises, magazine and television appearances and even her own commemorative stamp.

YACHTS OR LINERS?

Sporting four or five masts and 2000 square metres (21,000 square feet) of sails that can be unfurled in two minutes by a press of a button from the bridge, the ships of the WINDSTAR fleet are an unusual cross between contemporary cruise ships and traditional tall ships. With the sails continually adjusted by computers according to monitored wind speed and direction, greater precision and stability is achieved, although it is worth noting that the ships are propelled by their engines for at least half the time they are at sea.

Windstar Cruises

Founded by Scandinavian entrepreneurs Karl Andren and Jacob Stolt-Nielsen, Windstar Cruises introduced the first of a glamorous new breed of sail-cruisers in 1986. *Wind Star* was closely followed by two almost-identical sister ships, *Wind Song* and *Wind Spirit*, and joined by *Wind Surf*, formerly a Club Med sail-cruiser, in 1997. Windstar Cruises came under the massive umbrella of the Carnival Corporation in 1988, although Windstar's ships are still operated as a separate entity.

The line attracts a cosmopolitan mix of passengers drawn by friendly informality and unusual destinations in the Caribbean and Mediterranean. They also benefit from large, well-appointed cabins, 24-hour room service and open sitting dining with menus by celebrity chef Joachim Splichal. Entertainment is low-key, but there is live music for dancing and each vessel has a small casino, boutique, beauty salon, library and video selection for in-cabin viewing. Windstar ships are also noted for their sporting facilities, including a gymnasium, sauna and watersports platform with sailboats, windsurfers, Zodiacs, kayaks, and equipment for snorkelling, scuba diving, water-skiing and deep sea fishing. Above all, they have a luxurious 'private yacht' ambience with a high crew to passenger ratio.

Zeus Tours and Cruises

This 50 year-old company markets a fleet of small motorized sailing vessels, each with a capacity of between 26 and 49 passengers. Catering to a mainly north American clientele, these offbeat cruises spent island hopping throughout the Aegean are ideal for those wanting to discover the 'real' Greece and Turkey. Facilities are limited, but the ambience is lively and the cuisine is traditional Greek. Two of the fleet, *Lady Caterina* and *Pan Orama*, transfer to the Caribbean in the winter months.

Yacht Charter

Numerous companies all over the globe charter sailing vessels, complete with captain, crew and cook to do all the hard work. Alternatively, if you want to play an active role, you can hire a 'bareboat' and sail it yourself. Be aware, however, that to do this, you will have to prove your competency as sailors to the charterers. Passing a recognized course, such as those accredited by Britain's Royal Yachting Association or the American Sailing Association, should meet this requirement.

Information on chartering and charterers may be obtained from yachting schools and clubs, related magazines and organizations such as the American Sailing Association, Australian Yachting Federation, Irish Sailing Association, and the UK's Royal Yachting Association or Yacht Charter Association.

Planning a Yacht Charter

In choosing your region and charter company – and particularly if you intend renting bareboat – take into account the following considerations:

- **When is the best time to sail?** Peak season can result in crowded anchorages, and wind conditions and water temperatures may provide better sailing at less popular times of the year. In many parts of the Caribbean, for example, the best sailing weather comes in late spring.
- **What is the age and condition of the vessel?** Bareboats take some abusive handling and therefore deteriorate quicker than private vessels. Think twice about taking on a boat that is well over five years old.
- **What will I actually end up paying?** Charter prices vary enormously, and the rate for the same vessel may be twice as much in peak season as low season. Bear in mind too that hidden costs soon mount up. Your bareboat fee is unlikely to include charter taxes, provisioning, sporting options (such as windsurfers or dive gear) or insurance – a particularly necessary extra.

MEDICAL FACILITIES

In spite of a generally senior clientele, few river or coastal vessels have on-board medical facilities or a ship's doctor, although some crew members may have first aid training. They are also generally unsuitable for young children or disabled passengers. AS/CW's *Spirit of '98* does, however, feature an elevator and disabled cabins, CAPTAIN COOK CRUISES' *Murray Princess* has four disabled cabins and ACCL's *Niagara Prince* has a stair chair-lift. Be sure to check a ship's accessibility and ability to accommodate special requirements before booking.

RIVER AND COASTAL CRUISES

Going cruising doesn't mean you always have to stick to the high seas. Many companies visit some of the most famous and scenic waterways of the world, and while riverboats are generally smaller than most ocean-going cruise ships and offer proportionally fewer facilities and entertainment, they provide ideal surroundings in which to enjoy relaxed and relatively unstructured cruising. They are ideally suited to mature passengers who wish to explore the more rural, off-beat regions of their host country; those who enjoy a comfortable but unpretentious lifestyle; and those such as sea-sickness sufferers who are reluctant to take an ocean voyage.

Most riverboats carry between 100 and 200 passengers, although very modern vessels sometimes hold more (the *American Queen* takes over 430) and hotel barges, such as those that glide through the French canals, may carry far less (no more than 24 guests). In order to navigate the various types of waterway, whether they be canals or rivers, riverboats tend to be long, shallow-drafted and sufficiently low to pass under bridges that span their route. Riverboat **cabins** may be small and basic and on-board **cuisine** regional rather than gourmet, but travel is always at a leisurely pace, with plenty of time to stop at towns along the way and, unlike their ocean-going counterparts, the boats sail **by day**, so you don't miss passing points of interest – and, of course, you are usually much closer to them. In the evenings, guests are able to enjoy shore-side bars and restaurants or attend on-board shows provided by local entertainers.

Generally sheltered from extreme sea conditions, coastal voyages offer similar advantages to river journeys and, with an equally small passenger carry, also tend to be friendly and informal affairs, maybe incorporating an appropriate theme or activity such as fishing or whale-spotting.

The scope for exploring the rivers and inland waterways of the world is endless, but the major regions and operators of riverboat and coastal cruises are as follows:

RIVERBOAT MARKETING

Since European riverboats are frequently chartered or marketed by other travel companies, it is not uncommon to see the same vessel featured in the brochures of several totally unrelated tour operators.

Latin America: The Amazon

The massive Amazon region includes over 4800km (3000 miles) of river and is a dream destination for naturalists. Many mainstream cruise ships, including PRINCESS, P&O, FRED OLSEN, SEABOURN and SILVERSEA CRUISES, take in the delta and lower Amazon (from the port city of **Belém** to the jungle duty-free port of **Manaus**) in their South American itineraries. Smaller craft and specialist vessels, such as those of AMAZON TOURS & CRUISES and ABERCROMBIE & KENT'S *Explorer*, also venture beyond the wide reaches and along the more exotic tributaries and upper regions of this magnificent waterway (*see* Explorer Cruises).

North America

The **Mississippi** provides the most distinctive style of river cruising in North America in the shape of the throaty-whistled paddle steamers that once plied its waters in their hundreds. Today, the traditional fleet of the DELTA QUEEN STEAMBOAT COMPANY offers the ultimate all-American nostalgia trip along the Mississippi and neighbouring rivers of the Old South, with its sleepy towns, Civil War battlefields and plantation mansions.

In a similarly nostalgic vein, the recently formed AMERICAN WEST STEAMBOAT COMPANY operates a new reproduction paddle wheeler, *Queen of the West*, out of

Left: *The striking Victorian-style Mississippi riverboat* American Queen.

MISSISSIPPI MEANDERINGS

There are currently three steamers in the fleet of the DELTA QUEEN STEAMBOAT COMPANY – the genuine 1920s *Delta Queen* and the larger reproductions, *Mississippi Queen* and *American Queen*. An attractive blend of wholesome antiquity and modern convenience, each riverboat features Victorian-style decor and cabins, themed entertainment (including Dixieland Jazz and Riverboat shows), tasty Cajun cooking, an extensive shore excursion programme and facilities such as a gymnasium, gift shop, beauty salon and library. Rather more unusual cruise features include deck kite-flying, gentlemen escorts, lectures by a 'Riverlorian' (river historian) and the chance to play the calliope (the traditional steamship whistle-organ). Gamblers should note that, in spite of the poker-and-dice image perpetrated by old movies, these boats do not have a casino. They do, however, house regular theme cruises – the Kentucky Derby, American Civil War, Fall Foliage, Baseball, Christmas Bonfire and the annual Great Steamboat Race which culminates in St Louis every Fourth of July.

Portland, **Oregon**. This deluxe riverboat offers two to seven-night cruises on the **Columbia** and neighbouring west-coast rivers.

ST LAWRENCE CRUISE LINES operates five-, six- and seven-day cruises aboard the lovely replica steamboat, *Canadian Empress*. Scheduled from May to October, these leisurely trips afford relaxed sightseeing along the **St Lawrence** and **Ottawa** rivers.

If **Alaska** to you means wildlife rather than nightlife, you might prefer to shun the mega-ships in favour of the smaller vessels of GLACIER BAY TOURS AND CRUISES. This company offers educational cruises along the **Inside Passage** and **Glacier Bay** aboard a 50-passenger catamaran, *Executive Explorer*, and the smaller cruiser, *Wilderness Explorer*. WORLD EXPLORER CRUISES also offers a 14-day Alaskan adventure aboard the 800-passenger *Universe Explorer*.

The handsome fleet of ALASKA SIGHTSEEING/CRUISE WEST (AS/CW), offers a series of spectacular and unusual Alaskan itineraries. Sailing mostly from **Seattle**, these feature less-visited regions such as **El Capitan Passage**, **Sea Otter Sound**, **Admiralty Island**, **Desolation Sound**, **Princess Louisa Inlet** and other backwaters of the Inside Passage and Glacier Bay.

A similarly informal, destination-orientated programme is the focus of the AMERICAN CANADIAN CARIBBEAN LINE (ACCL). Offering what they call 'uncommon, unhurried and unspoiled' river and coastal itineraries around the more secluded waters of the **Bahamas**, **Virgin Islands**, **Belize**, **Aruba**, **Bonaire** and **Curaçao**, this unpretentious line boasts a high percentage of repeat guests. Further north, ACCL's *Mayan Prince* follows an itinerary that includes **Rhode Island**, **Long Island Sound**, the **Hudson River**, **Lake Ontario** and **Saguenay Fjord**. The *Niagara Prince* follows a scenic route along the **Mobile, Tennessee**, **Mississippi** and **Illinois rivers**, the **Tenn-Tom Waterway**, the **Great Lakes** and **Erie Canal**.

CLIPPER CRUISE LINE have similarly personable all-American crews and high numbers of repeat guests for

EXPLORING THE WATERWAYS OF NORTH AMERICA

When not exploring Canadian and Alaskan waters, AS/CW's *Spirit of '98* crosses the dams and locks of the **Columbia** and **Snake rivers** between Portland and the Idaho border; *Spirit of Alaska* follows the **Sacramento** and **Napa rivers** from Sausalito through Gold Rush and wine-growing country; and *Spirit of Columbia* navigates the scenic **Columbia River Gorge** and locks of the **Bonneville Dam**.

EXPLORING TECHNOLOGY

Designed and built by the line's adventurous founder, **Luther Blount**, ACCL's cruisers have a number of distinctive features, including patented **bow ramps** that allow easy access at otherwise difficult anchorages. Other features make certain trips feasible, such as a **retractable wheelhouse** or, in the case of the *Niagara Prince*, a unique **ballasting** system that submerges the hull an extra 25cm (10in), to allow passage under Chicago's low bridges. The line's newest addition – the slightly larger, 100-passenger *Grande Caribe* – has been fitted with **stabilizers** in order to undertake voyages to Newfoundland and around Canada's eastern coast.

their 102-passenger *Nantucket Clipper*, 138-passenger *Yorktown Clipper* and 118-passenger *Clipper Adventurer*. Their itineraries include in-depth cruises along both the **east** and **west coasts** of the USA, Mexico's **Sea of Cortez**, Alaska's **Inside Passage**, the Pacific northwest's **San Juan** and **Gulf Islands** and off-beat regions of the 'real' **Caribbean**. These vessels also explore such diverse waterways as the **Columbia** and **Sacramento rivers**, **Panama Canal**, **St Lawrence Seaway** and Venezuela's **Orinoco**.

A recent addition to upscale cruising on the **St Lawrence** and **Great Lakes** between Montreal and Chicago is HAPAG-LLOYD'S 14,000grt *Columbus* – a deluxe, contemporary vessel, catering to a maximum of 420 predominantly German-speaking passengers.

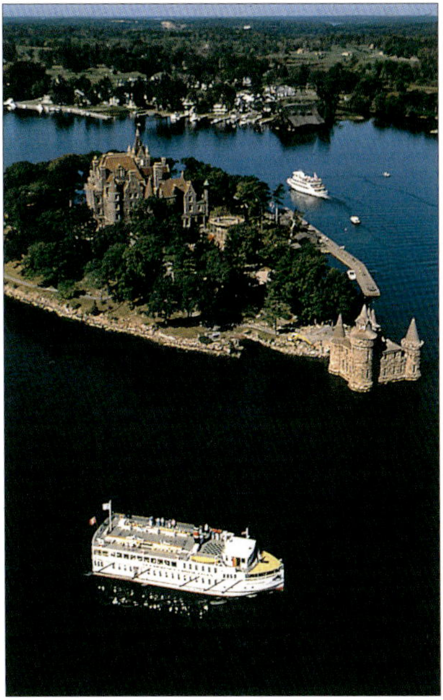

Above: *St Lawrence riverboat* Canadian Empress.

Northern Europe: Scandinavia

There can be few better ways to explore the Land of the Midnight Sun than from the decks of the mail delivery ships that ply the craggy Norwegian coast. Known locally as **Hurtigruten** or 'fast route' (marketed in the USA as **Bergen Line**), these hardy vessels not only transport mail, but cars and machinery, fresh and frozen produce, local commuters and residents of remote settlements, for whom the regular year-round service is a lifeline. They also carry tourists on cruises of up to 11 days from **Bergen** to **Kirkenes**, calling at over 30 small communities en route. They sail to a strict schedule, with time in port varying from 15 minutes to several hours, but shore excursions and overland options to rejoin the cruise are available.

The coastal voyage fleet is divided into three groups: traditional, mid-generation and new ships. The traditional ships (*Harald Jarl*, *Lofoten*) are now over 30 years

WORDS OF WISDOM

CLIPPER CRUISES veer towards the upper end of the price scale, promoting an intimate, intellectual ambience in a comfortable, but not budget, setting. Their lecture programme is particularly strong, with cruises divided into **Classic Editions** (focusing on the cultural and historical aspects of the route with lectures by accompanying experts) and **Adventure Editions** (focusing on nature and wildlife and accompanied by the line's own scientists and naturalists).

Above: *The coastal cruiser* Narvik *in Trollfjord in northern Norway.*

old and nearing the end of their service. Although they lack many of the facilities of their more modern counterparts (accommodation is particularly basic), these old workhorses are still the unquestionable choice of romantics and nautical enthusiasts. The mid-generation ships (*Midnatsol, Narvik* and *Vesterålen*) were built in the 1980s and each carry over 300 passengers and up to 40 cars, whilst the newer ships (*Kong Harald, Nordlys, Richard With, Nordkapp, Polarlys* and *Nordnorge*) have increased capacities of 490 berths and space for 50 cars. The new and mid-generation ships have elevators and disability cabins.

It is not only the spectacular beauty of the Norwegian fjords that attracts visitors to northern Europe. The scenic archipelago off the coast of **Sweden** and the coasts of **Finland** and **Estonia** are also destinations for many of the region's ultra-modern ferry services. These vessels traverse northern European waters long after the mainstream cruise ships have left for milder climes and are regularly included in tour/cruise programmes of travel companies such as **Eurocruises**. Specific ferry information may be obtained from regional tourist boards.

The Finnish family-owned KRISTINA CRUISES operates the petite *Kristina Regina* (1960) – a twin-funnelled vessel that spends her time cruising Scandinavia's scenic coastal waters. With up to 350 passengers, this is high-density cruising, but in charming, convivial, old-world surroundings.

SEEKING THE LIGHT

To avoid rough winter seas and experience the **continuous daylight** for which the region is famed, the Hurtigruten journey up the Norwegian coast is ideally made between mid-May and late July. But those hoping to witness the spectacular celestial phenomenon, the **Aurora Borealis** (Northern Lights), should plan their voyage between mid-November and mid-January.

Northern Europe: The British Isles

Above: *The cosy interior of* Hebridean Princess.

For those seeking a truly unique cruise experience, HEBRIDEAN ISLAND CRUISES offers a rare treat aboard the *Hebridean Princess*. A floating version of a comfortable rustic inn (complete with wing-chairs and brick fireplace!), this charming coastal vessel provides superb Scottish fare and excellent service from an all-British crew. Her cabins (including 10 singles) are individually designed with authentic touches of Victoriana and rates include the use of boats, bicycles and fishing gear, entrance fees to local attractions and the services of specialist guides. *Hebridean Princess* carries approximately 50 passengers on wide-ranging British coastal cruises which include the **Orkney** and **Hebridean islands**.

Explorer vessels, such as HAPAG-LLOYD'S *Hanseatic*, SPECIAL EXPEDITIONS' *Polaris* and MARINE EXPEDITIONS' *Marine Discovery*, include the British Isles in their coastal itineraries. Numerous ferries also ply the English Channel, Irish Sea and North Sea, linking coastal Britain with Ireland, continental Europe and the off-lying Shetlands, Orkneys, Isle of Man and Channel Islands.

> **THE WAVERLEY**
>
> Although not offering overnight accommodation, the amazing 50 year-old coastal vessel, *Waverley*, is worth noting as 'the last sea-going paddle steamer in the world'. Owned by the Paddle Steamer Preservation Society and operated by WAVERLEY EXCURSIONS, *Waverley* and the classic pleasure cruise ship (and survivor of Campbell's White Funnel fleet) *Balmoral*, tour the coasts of England, Wales, Ireland, Scotland and the Isle of Man.

European Inland Waterways

From the fairy-tale castles of the **Rhine** to the lush greenery of **Ireland** or the forests of deepest **Russia**, Europe offers by far the most extensive range of the world's river cruises. Most European riverboats operate annually between March and October, with peak season in July and August (although late May and early September are often the most attractive times to go).

One of the oldest companies to operate such cruises is KD DEUTSCHE FLUSSKREUZFAHRTEN. Formed in 1826, this

THE GÖTA CANAL

For those seeking a unique introduction to Sweden, the **Göta Canal**, with thousands of islands and 65 locks, is plied by the three characterful steamers of the GÖTA CANAL STEAMSHIP COMPANY. Offering plenty of stops during their four-day (and occasional six-day) sailings between **Gothenburg** and **Stockholm**, these vintage vessels provide a leisurely transit, evocative of a bygone age. They are marketed by Eurocruises, Bergen Line and Strand Voyages.

company offers itineraries on waterways including the rivers **Rhine**, **Moselle**, **Elbe**, **Danube**, **Rhône** and **Seine**. Sailings on the recently completed **Rhine-Main-Danube Canal** and on the **Neva-Volga** between St Petersburg and Moscow have also been introduced. Carrying between 100 and 200 guests in comfortable surroundings, this large fleet of modern vessels provides an enviable way to approach historic cities such as **Amsterdam**, **Prague**, **Vienna** and **Budapest**.

DEILMANN REEDEREI (PETER DEILMANN RIVER & OCEAN CRUISES) offers a truly luxurious riverboat experience on some of Europe's favourite waterways. On the **Danube**, **Elbe**, **Rhine**, **Rhône** and **Saône** the *Mozart*, *Prussian Princess*, *Dresden Princess*, *Princesse de Provence*, *Danube Princess* and elegant *River Cloud* wend their way through Germany, Belgium, Holland, Austria, Slovakia, Hungary, Romania, Bulgaria and France.

Other operators of central and eastern European river cruises include SWAN HELLENIC, PHOENIX REISEN, SAGA CRUISES and EUROPE CRUISE LINE. The latter also offers sailings between **Amsterdam** and **Stettin** in Poland (taking in the German cities of **Hamburg** and **Berlin**) aboard the *Diana* – which has a hydraulically

Below: *A riverboat from the large KD DEUTSCHE FLUSSLREUZFAHRTEN fleet docked in Cologne.*

Left: *The easy pace and idyllic countryside of barge-cruising on the French canals.*

lowered wheelhouse allowing navigation beneath the low bridges on its route.

LEISURE CRUISES of Switzerland (marketed in the UK by VOYAGES JULES VERNE) offers cruises on the **Seine** and **Saône**, the **Danube**, the **Douro** in Portugal, the **Po** in Italy (taking in **Venice** and **Verona**), the **Yenisei** in Siberia (reaching the Arctic Ocean), the **Dnieper** (through Ukraine from **Kiev** to the **Black Sea**) and **Neva**, **Svir** and **Volga** waterways in Russia. The British operator, NOBLE CALEDONIA, the AMERICAN ODESSAMERICA CRUISE COMPANY and EUROCRUISES also market Russian river cruises between **Moscow** and **St Petersburg**, sometimes incorporating classical music or cultural themes.

Africa: The Nile

The fact that Upper and Lower Egypt is denoted by the source of the Nile and not the points of the compass (Upper Egypt is to the south and Lower Egypt to the north) shows the inherent significance of the world's longest river on the land through which it flows. Even today, most of the country's vast population clusters along its fertile banks, which are toiled according to age-old traditions.

In the company of innumerable *feluccas* (traditional sailboats sometimes used for short pleasure trips), approximately 150 riverboats ply the Nile. Most of the

BARGE HOLIDAYS

One of the most popular ways to explore the British Isles or France is by traditional steel narrowboat or barge – chugging in the gentle wake of their working ancestors, gliding under stone bridges, past grazing cattle, mooring at rural villages and waterside inns. Carrying few passengers and providing cosy accommodation (they aren't called narrowboats for nothing!), they offer an even more intimate and unstructured cruise experience than that of their larger river cruise counterparts. While some of these vessels come complete with captain and cook, others are available for you to hire and manage yourself. ABERCROMBIE & KENT is among the forerunners of European hotel-boat operators, while other British and French riverboats are marketed by Blakes Boating Holidays, Cruise Company of Greenwich, Drifters Hotel Boats, European Waterways, French Country Waterways, Le Boat and UK Waterway Holidays. Numerous regional operators also advertise in boating magazines.

THE NILE: WHEN TO GO

Nile cruise prices vary enormously between low season (June–August) and high season (October–April). The advantage of low season prices, however, is easily offset by a summer heat and dust that can make sightseeing unbearable. Even during the mellower months between September and May, excursions are restricted to early morning and late afternoon.

Above: *Slipping through Egypt's ancient history aboard the Nile riverboat* Queen Nabila.

bigger, newer vessels (such as those operated by international hotel chains) are in the style of the European riverboats, with comfortable air-conditioned cabins and amenities such as a sun deck, swimming pool, beauty salon, laundry, inclusive shore excursions and the services of specialist historians and guides.

For most travellers, the journey begins in **Aswan** and ends at **Luxor** (or vice-vesa) and includes visits to ancient **Thebes**, **Karnak** and the **Valley of the Kings**. These cruises, which are usually part of a more extensive sightseeing schedule, last four or five days, although longer options are available, including 12-day itineraries between Luxor and **Cairo**. At the time of writing, however, SWAN HELLENIC's *Nile Monarch* is the only luxury boat to offer regular high season cruises between upper Egypt and the modern capital.

Numerous travel companies include Nile cruises in their packages, with principal operators including ABERCROMBIE & KENT, HILTON INTERNATIONAL NILE CRUISES, NABILA NILE CRUISES, OBEROI NILE CRUISES, PRESIDENTIAL NILE CRUISES, SHERATON NILE CRUISES, SONESTA HOTELS and SWAN HELLENIC CRUISES.

HISTORY ON THE NILE

Nostalgia buffs may be interested to note two historic paddle steamers among the various Nile vessels marketed by VOYAGES JULES VERNE. The *SS Karim* was originally built for King Fouad, was inherited by King Farouk and then later used by presidents Nasser and Sadat, while the *SS Mahasen* was built for King Fouad's government ministers and is the sister vessel of the *Memnon* – the floating star of *Death on the Nile*. Voyages Jules Verne also markets the paddle steamer-style *Kariba Belle* on Zimbabwe's Lake Kariba.

Asia: The Yangtze

The great central waterway of China, the Yangtze (known in Chinese as Changjiang, meaning 'long river') has had tourist cruises in increasingly well-equipped riverboats since the early 1980s. The modern, 150 plus-passenger vessels that currently ply these waters typically offer a choice of western and eastern cuisine, observation and sun decks, a swimming pool, library, bars, health facilities (gym, sauna, massage) and even conference rooms or business centres. Most have Chinese officers and crew members and karaoke is the principal entertainment feature. Leisure programmes may include acupuncture, qigong, t'ai chi and displays of folk art, martial arts and Chinese theatre.

Most Yangtze cruises follow the river between **Wuhan** and **Chongqing** on a leisurely four- or five-night journey through the **Xiling**, **Wu** and **Qutang Gorges** (The Three Gorges). A frequent and worthwhile detour also incorporates the dramatic scenery of the **Three Lesser Gorges** of the **Da-Ning River**. Three-night cruises tend to omit the latter and the section of river between Shashi and Chongqing.

Major operators of Yangtze River cruises include ABERCROMBIE & KENT, CHINA YANGTZE RIVER SHIPPING COMPANY, HOLIDAY INN/ASIA PACIFIC, REGAL CHINA CRUISES, and VICTORIA CRUISES. Numerous travel companies – including the many international offices of the China Travel Service – also feature Yangtze cruises in their general Chinese programmes.

Left: *A ferry boat on the Yangtze at the bustling port of Shanghai.*

THE YANGTZE: WHEN TO GO

The cruising season extends from late February to early December, but low water levels can affect end-of-season itineraries and July and August can be unbearably hot. Arguably, the best time to visit is May or September.

THE FLOODING OF XILING GORGE

A Yangtze cruise is not without its poignancy, for even as this book goes to press, the construction of the massive Three Gorges Dam at **Sandouping**, due for completion in 2009, is changing the face of the river forever. Its gigantic wall will contain a lake of over 644 square kilometres (400 square miles), indundating most of the Xiling Gorge, flooding the landscape and historic temples and forcing the evacuation of over a million inhabitants. While supporters of the project stress the energy benefits – 85 billion kilowatt hours produced annually – that will be generated for Shanghai and the Lower Yangtze Basin, opponents decry the destruction of a significant section of China's natural environment, heritage and culture.

Above: *VSOE's luxurious* Road to Mandalay *on a cruise up the Ayeyarwady River in Myanmar.*

Myanmar: River Ayeyarwady

Rudyard Kipling dubbed Burma's Irrawaddy River 'The Road to Mandalay' and, in spite of a couple of name changes (Burma is now Myanmar and the Irrawaddy is the Ayeyarwady), this famous waterway is now home to the appropriately named *Road to Mandalay* riverboat. She is operated by VENICE SIMPLON ORIENT EXPRESS (VSOE) and a two- to seven-night cruise (**Bagan** to/from **Mandalay**) may be combined with a passage on the prestigious Eastern & Oriental Express train. With only 20 passengers, *Myat Thanda* is a smaller riverboat, but sails a longer course (between **Prome** and Mandalay). Operated by the SCOTTISH IRRAWADDY FLOTILLA COMPANY, she is marketed by NOBLE CALEDONIA and ESPLANADE TOURS.

> **FINDING TASSIE**
>
> With regular scheduled sailings between mainland Australia (**Melbourne**) and the island of Tasmania (**Devonport**), TT-LINE's *Spirit of Tasmania* is a ship with a difference. An insight into the state's history and culture is provided by a unique on-board Visitor Centre with displays and video presentations, a tourist information bureau and suites honouring Tasmanian celebrities.

Australia: Murray River

One of the world's longest rivers, Australia's Murray River rises in the Great Dividing Range and flows between the twin cities of **Albury** and **Wodonga** on its journey to the Indian Ocean near **Adelaide**. Recreating the days of the settlers and pioneers, paddlewheelers still churn these waters, offering short pleasure trips past the region's sandstone cliffs and gum forests. The largest of these paddlewheelers is CAPTAIN COOK CRUISES' *Murray Princess* – a well-appointed 120-passenger vessel that sails between **Mannum** and **Morgan**, taking in the **Barossa wine-growing region**, **Ngaut Ngaut Conservation Park**, **Punyelroo Caves**, speedboat rides and a traditional campfire and bushdance. PROUD AUSTRALIA HOLIDAYS' smaller *Proud Mary* also offers Murray River cruises, with the emphasis on eco-tourism and including guided bush walks and nocturnal tours.

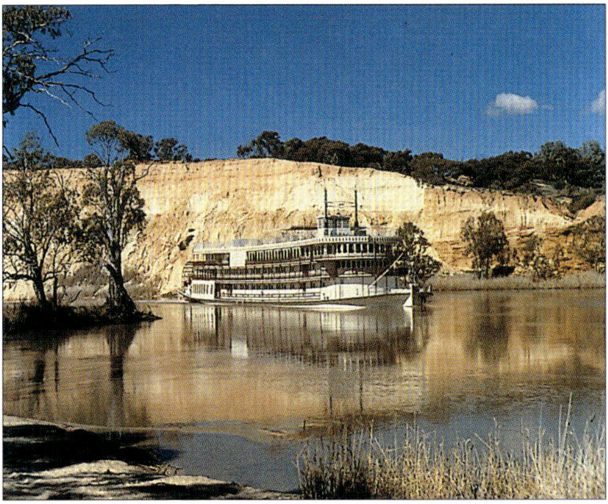

Left: *The paddlewheeler* Murray Princess *cruising the dry, empty reaches of Australia's Murray River.*

Coastal Australasia and the South Pacific

The turquoise seas of Australasia tend to be ignored by most of the major cruise lines – mostly because of the region's distance from the main cruise markets, the USA and Europe. But the big ships' loss is the small ships' gain and yachts and cruisers of all descriptions enjoy some wonderful sailing in the coastal waters of **Australia** and **New Zealand**.

Alongside the numerous sailboat and yacht operators (*see* Sailing Ships and Yachts), CAPTAIN COOK CRUISES offers three-, four- and seven-night voyages out of **Cairns** to the magnificent **Great Barrier Reef** aboard the 168-passenger vessel, *Reef Endeavour*. Among the facilities aboard are a glass bottom boat, snorkelling/dive tenders and a resident marine naturalist and dive master.

ROYLEN CRUISES operates two- to five-day itineraries out of **Mackay** and **Hamilton Island** aboard the *Roylen Endeavour* and *Roylen Endeavour II*, each carrying around 50 passengers. Beautiful uninhabited islands are interspersed with visits to well-equipped resorts such as **Brampton** and **Daydream**.

The 54-passenger catamarans of CORAL PRINCESS CRUISES also explore the Great Barrier Reef, with departures from **Cairns** or **Townsville**. Itineraries include **Hinchinbrook Channel**, **Dunk Island** and the company's

CRUISING FIJI

The CAPTAIN COOK CRUISES fleet includes several small deluxe vessels sailing out of **Sydney** and two tall ships sailing out of **Nadi**, Fiji. The former *Reef Escape* also goes island-hopping around Fiji's **Mamanuca** and **Yasawa islands** as the *Dro Ki Cakau* (Fijian for 'Reef Escape'). BLUE LAGOON CRUISES' modern fleet of motor yachts – including the beautiful 72-passenger 'flagship', *Mystique Princess* – also hugs the palm-fringed coastlines of the scenic Mamanuca and Yasawa islands. Founded in 1950 by New Zealand captain Trevor Withers and Australian aviator Harold Gatty, this Fiji-based company offers varying short cruises of up to a week's duration, incorporating water-sports (such as snorkelling and sailboarding), glass-bottom boat trips and traditional folk-lore, entertainment and wonderful 'Lovo' feasts.

Above: *A chance to explore northern Queensland's tropical coast with* CORAL PRINCESS CRUISES.

exclusive, coral-fringed, **Pelorus Island**. Scuba diving tuition is available, together with snorkel equipment, a glass bottom boat and a comprehensive reference library. This company also offers expedition-style cruises across the top of Australia from Cairns to **Darwin** and around the rivers and inlets of **The Kimberley**, starting at either **Broome** or Darwin.

Other itineraries include NIUGINI CRUISES' *Sepik Spirit*, which not only explores coastal Australia but also cruises around its base island of **Papua New Guinea**; GREAT ADVENTURES, OCEAN SPIRIT CRUISES, QUICKSILVER CONNECTIONS and PURE PLEASURE CRUISES, which offer short sailings to reefs and islands; MIRIMAR CRUISES, with daily trips to Brisbane's **Lone Pine Koala Sanctuary**; and KANGAROO EXPLORER'S four- to seven-day snorkelling, fishing and diving cruises to **Lizard Island**, **Cooktown**, the **Cod Hole**, marketed as part of the **Cape York** safari packages offered by Australian travel company WILDERNESS CHALLENGE.

DISCOVERING ANTARCTICA

Few passenger explorer ships venture beyond the Antarctic Peninsula, although ORIENT LINES' *Marco Polo* and QUARK EXPEDITIONS' *Kapitan Khlebnikov* are notable exceptions. The latter – a Russian ice-breaker, chartered from Murmansk Shipping – successfully completed both a semi-navigation and the first ever tourist circumnavigation of the Antarctic continent in January 1997. QUARK also offers a voyage around the far side of Antarctica, starting and finishing in **Australia**. In a bid to repeat its successful Antarctic exercise in the Northern hemisphere, QUARK is planning a circumnavigation of the Arctic Circle aboard the *Kapitan Dranitsyn*.

EXPLORER CRUISING

Explorer ships sail quite literally to the ends of the earth in search of off-beat destinations and unique ecosystems. **Antarctica** and the far reaches of the **Amazon** are particularly popular regions, followed by the **Galápagos Islands**, the **Arctic Circle** and coastal **Central America**.

Explorer vessels, by the very nature of their adventures, are noticeably different to mainstream cruise ships. Those venturing into pack ice are built with specially reinforced hulls, those navigating rivers and tributaries will invariably be smaller and those moving in coastal waters have a suitably shallow draft. Shipboard personnel may include regional **specialists** such as expert lecturers in relevant disciplines or Zodiac pilots with experience of polar navigation. There will be little or no on-board entertainment and library facilities will house primarily destination-related material.

Passengers aboard explorer ships tend to be adventurous, academic and relatively active (bearing in mind that sightseeing can be strenuous and Zodiacs are often used for transportation). On explorer vessels, the attire is distinctly practical, the on-board ambience relaxed and the passenger carry low.

ANTARCTIC WHEN TO GO

Cruises to the Great White Continent are traditionally scheduled between **November and February**, when the pack ice has receded and wildlife is most abundant. December and January are the **warmest** months with temperatures hovering around freezing point, although February is the best month for **whale-spotting**.

Antarctica

Most Antarctic cruises depart from **Ushaia** in Chile – the southernmost city in the world – and encompass **Drake Passage**, the **Antarctic Peninsula** and possibly the **Falkland Islands**, **South Georgia**, **South Orkney Islands** and **South Shetland Islands**. Although always subject to weather conditions, regular highlights include the flooded caldera of Deception Island, the research station of **Half Moon Island**, the spectacular **Lemaire Channel** and the penguin rookeries of islands such as **Livingston** and **King George**.

The Russian ice-breakers of MARINE EXPEDITIONS and SOUTHERN HERITAGE EXPEDITIONS, HAPAG-LLOYD'S deluxe *Hanseatic* and *Bremen*, SOCIETY EXPEDITIONS' elegant *World Discover*, ABERCROMBIE & KENT'S cheery little *Explorer* and NOBLE CALEDONIA'S ever-popular *Caledonian Star* all offer explorer cruises in Antarctic waters.

Below: *The ice-breaker* Kapitan Khlebnikov *tackles the ice floes of the Ross Sea in Antarctica.*

The Amazon

Many vessels, including quite large cruise ships, sail approximately 1600km (1000 miles) along this mighty river from Brazil's delta port of **Belém** to its jungle port of **Manaus** (*see* River and Coastal Cruises). Expedition ships, however, use Zodiacs to explore the tributaries – as the main reaches are up to 50km (30 miles) wide, this is the only way to appreciate the magnificent wildlife and plantlife of the basin.

MARINE EXPEDITIONS, SPECIAL EXPEDITIONS and ABERCROMBIE & KENT offer itineraries between Belém and Iquitos, while AMAZON TOURS & CRUISES operates several small vessels manned by Peruvian crews in a range of two- to six-night adventures from Iquitos and Leticia.

AMAZING AMAZONIA

The tributaries **Rio Pucuri** and **Rio Curua** provide excellent bird watching, while the **Lago Carauaçu** is famed for its two species of freshwater dolphins. Beyond **Manaus**, the river becomes narrower and takes on more of its classical associations – the stilt homes of jungle dwellers, three-toed sloths, parrots, monkeys and rare plants (such as the *Victoria Amazonica* – the world's largest waterlily) can be spied en route to the Peruvian frontier town of **Iquitos**, the farthest navigable point.

The Galápagos Islands

A haven for rare animals and plantlife and a place intimately connected with Charles Darwin's *The Origin of Species*, this group of 15 equatorial islands is a naturalist's dream. **Hood** and **Tower islands**, for example, are home to the frosty-headed marine iguana and blue- and red-footed boobies; **Floreana Island** is surrounded by exquisite corals and tropical fish; **James Island** is famed for its birds (including the Galápagos hawk); **South Plaza Island** has iguanas and sea lions; and **Isabel Island** plays host to the region's famous giant tortoises.

DIRIGO CRUISES offers island-hopping out of San Christobal aboard the 18-passenger trimaran, *Lammer Law*, INCA FLOATS operates year-round expeditions here and various adventure tour operators (including WILDERNESS TRAVEL, ODESSAMERICA and NOBLE

CALEDONIA) offer Galápagos itineraries in conjunction with owners of local vessels (such as GALÁPAGOS CRUISES). These are often advertised in natural history and travel-related newspapers and magazines.

Above: *The 20,000grt QUARK EXPEDITIONS explorer ship* Yamal.
Opposite: *An inflatable Zodiac transfers passengers on an ABERCROMBIE & KENT Amazon explorer cruise to their ship.*

The Arctic Circle

Humpback and beluga whales, Arctic foxes and polar bears, the eponymous inhabitants of **Walrus Island**, the world's fastest moving glacier (**Jakobshavn**), the Norse ruins of **Hvalsey**, **Greenland**'s hot springs, the geology of **Gros Morne**, the icebergs of **Disco Bay**, the seabirds of the **Bering Strait** and **Digges Island** are all highlights of Arctic expeditions, whose range extends from northern Europe to northern Canada.

Many of the vessels that explore the Antarctic between November and February head north to the Arctic between June and September. These include the ice-breakers of MARINE EXPEDITIONS, SPECIAL EXPEDITIONS, HAPAG-LLOYD and QUARK EXPEDITIONS. The Norwegian ships of SVALBARD POLAR TRAVEL venture to northerly extremes and specialist regional tour operators also include expedition-style voyages as part of inclusive packages.

Coastal South and Central America

Lush rainforests and ecologically interesting islands, such as Costa Rica's **Golfo de Chiriqui** and **Isla de Coiba**, contribute to Latin America's popularity as an explorer destination. The **Chilean Fjords** offer the fabled island of **Chiloé**, the hanging glacier and black-necked swans of **Laguna San Rafael** and the seals, penguins and flamingoes of **Torres del Paine National Park**. A wealth of unspoiled natural beauty is also provided by the islands of Mexico's **Sea of Cortez**, including at least 60 species of cactus and other plants endemic to the region. March is a particularly good month to spot blue whales in these waters.

PROTECTING NATURE

A zealously-guarded province of Ecuador, Ecuadorean-registered ships have priority in the Galápagos Islands, which is why expedition operators usually charter local vessels. Strict visitors' guidelines apply: no smoking, touching wildlife, collecting native items (such as plants and rocks) or wandering off the trails. All passengers are escorted ashore in small groups by guides.

Environmentally friendly Expeditions

Eco-tourism is, of course, a key factor behind all explorer cruises. The Antarctic Conservation Act of 1978 expressly forbids the removal or introduction of species, the unauthorized discharge or disposal of pollutants and the capture, harassment or attempt to harm native wildlife. Other environmentally sensitive regions are enforcing similar rulings and expedition vessels are aiming to meet 'zero discharge' levels. It is to be hoped that all cruise vessels will follow suit.

Special Expeditions visits Costa Rica and circumnavigates the **Baja California Peninsula** via the Sea of Cortez; Temptress Cruises (marketed by the Cruise Company of Greenwich), Cruceros Australis (marketed by OdessAmerica and Noble Caledonia), Society Expeditions and Hapag-Lloyd sail the Costa Rican, Chilean and other Latin American coastlines; and World Explorer Cruises offers Latin American winter expeditions and heads for Alaska in the summer.

Unusual and One-Off Voyages

Canal Transits

Some sea-going cruises may include a transit of a canal or other waterway, which should be treated as a day at sea (don't expect to be able to get off the ship). Canal transits are often a cruise highlight with, perhaps, a lecturer's narration of points of interest broadcast over the open decks. Wherever possible, passenger ship transits are scheduled during daylight hours, although your vessel may have to wait to join a convoy of other ships for the passage.

There are four principal canals in the world commonly used by cruise ships. The **Corinth Canal**, built between 1882 and 1893, links the Ionian and Aegean seas and divides the Peloponnese from the rest of mainland Greece. It is too narrow to accommodate large ships but its sheer walls provide an impressive 'short cut' for vessels of up to approximately 12,000grt. Whether by day or night (the canal looks equally impressive by floodlight) the transit lasts little more than one hour. Completed in 1895, the **Kiel Canal** cuts across northern Germany to link the Baltic to the North Sea. It runs for approximately 96km (60 miles) between the town of Kiel and the mouth of

Below: *The dramatic cut of the nineteenth-century Corinth Canal.*

Above: *PRINCESS CRUISES'* Royal Princess *navigates through the Panama Canal.*

the River Elbe and is sufficiently wide (45m/148ft) and deep (14m/46ft) to accommodate most mid-sized passenger vessels. Transit times average seven to eight hours.

The **Panama Canal** – with its locks, lakes, locomotive 'mules' (to guide ships in transit) and Puente de las Americas (Bridge of the Americas) – is a particularly interesting waterway that deserves a place on the 'hit list' of every keen traveller. Completed in 1914, and cutting across the isthmus of Panama to link the Pacific and Atlantic Oceans, it is 82km (51 miles) long, up to 300m (980ft) wide, 100m (330ft) deep, and takes approximately nine hours to transit.

Opened in 1869, the **Suez Canal** is the vital link between the Mediterranean and the Red Sea. It runs 173km (107 miles) from Port Said to Port Suez and is able to carry even the largest cruise ships with ease. With few points of interest, however, other than desert memorials and rusting reminders of the Arab-Israeli Six-Day War, the Suez Canal holds less attraction for the visitor than the Panama. The average transit takes between 12 and 18 hours, depending on the convoy system.

A CORINTHIAN ACHIEVEMENT

The idea of a canal across the narrow isthmus between the Ionian and Aegean seas where the Peloponnese peninsula connects to the Greek mainland was first championed by the Roman emperor **Nero**. While the actual canal was built only in the late nineteenth century, cruise ship passengers can still get a flavour of Roman life at the ancient city of **Corinth**, a few kilometres beyond **Kórinthos** (modern Corinth). The Romans chose Corinth rather than Athens as the capital of Greece, and the city once had a population of three quarters of a million.

THE EIGHTY-FIRST DAY

Like Phileas Fogg in Jules Verne's famous globe-trotting adventure *Around the World in 80 Days*, some passengers on a circumnavigation forget that you lose (or gain) a day on the way round! Passing through different time zones as your ship circumnavigates the globe means you officially 'lose' a day going westwards and 'gain' a day going eastwards. Most passengers prefer, however, to follow a westerly route as the regular time changes mean the clocks are always retarded, rather than advanced.

Maiden Voyages

There is always a certain excitement about being among the first to do anything – and being part of the action on a brand new vessel is no exception. Some very tempting deals are offered on inaugural cruises, whether maiden voyages, '**shake-down**' cruises or those directly after a ship has been refurbished. (The official maiden voyage is not necessarily a ship's very first trip, as there may have been one or two previous 'shake-down' or trial cruises.) Such prices, however, are usually offered in anticipation of all the things that can – and sometimes do – go wrong. In the first instance, **shipyard problems** (strikes, financial setbacks, lack of completion etc.) can delay the sailing of the vessel and result in the first few cruises being cancelled or postponed. Even if the ship does sail on time, it may experience **teething trouble** – plumbing and electrical faults, missing or misplaced stores and supplies, and inadequate service from crew members who are as lost around the ship as you are!

Repositioning Cruises

As the title implies, repositioning cruises are those by which vessels move from one cruising region to another. Ships that sail in two or more different parts of the globe according to season are likely to offer repositioning cruises at least twice yearly, normally in March/April and October/November. They are rarely advertised as such, but if you see an itinerary listed that is markedly different from those regularly offered by that vessel, chances are it is a repositioning cruise. If the journey is lengthy, it may even be divided into two or three separate cruises.

The advantages of repositioning cruises are

Opposite and above: *Life aboard the* QE2*, which offers regular transatlantic crossings and an annual world cruise.*

that they may incorporate rarely visited ports, that due to the sheer distances involved they tend to be longer than average and include a higher ratio of days at sea, making for a generally more relaxing trip, and that cruise lines often offer very good deals on such cruises. On the other hand, *because* the ports are less-frequented, there may be hitches concerning supplies and shore excursions, and low-season sailings also mean potentially unpredictable weather and sea conditions.

World Cruises

The ambition of every lottery-winner and would-be billionaire, a world cruise is regarded as the epitome of luxury travel. But beyond the hyperbole, and presuming that time and money are no object, it is worth considering how suitable such a cruise is for your personal tastes. World cruises are usually scheduled to begin in January and last approximately **three months**. While they circumnavigate the globe (and this usually includes at least one or two equator crossings), they invariably leave whole land masses untouched. In addition, they are not

Transatlantic Crossings

In spite of the demise of the great liners and the growth of the airline industry, it is still possible to cross the Atlantic by cruise ship. Various lines offer transatlantic crossings between Europe and the Americas, often including Madeira, the Canary Islands, the Bahamas or Azores on the lengthier, yet climatically kinder, southerly route. Only Cunard's *Queen Elizabeth 2* currently offers a regular transatlantic service across the traditional northern route.

Above: *'The Queen' – the ultimate world cruiser.*

port-intensive – while you could be visiting 40 destinations, there will be a lot of **days at sea**, which will suit those preferring a more relaxed passage, although boredom can creep in. They generally attract a more **mature** clientele and certainly allow plenty of time and opportunities to get to know your fellow guests. Friendships and romances regularly develop during those long months at sea.

There is always a special **atmosphere** about a world cruise. The ship often generates local interest and is greeted by bands or performers on the pierside, and when a famous vessel such as the *QE2*, comes into port, she's guaranteed to be the star attraction. As a result, world cruises tend to be more glamorous – and formal – than others. This means a lot of 'black tie' nights, gala dinners and cocktail parties. If you prefer a more unusual – and less 'dressy' – experience, world cruises are offered by some **passenger-cargo companies** as well as the big cruise liners. By the same token, if you *do* want to sample the unique world-cruise ambience but don't want to go all the way, it is almost always possible to do a **section** of a circumnavigation.

Despite the prestige attached to them, world cruises are rarely fully booked, and it is nearly always possible to obtain good last-minute deals. However, don't jump in at the deep end. Never spend your life savings, lucky windfall or sudden inheritance on a full world circumnavigation if you have never taken a cruise before. Always test the water first – and preferably on the same ship (and in the same grade of cabin) that you intend for your global voyage. A 10- to 14-day cruise on your chosen vessel should give you a good taster of cruising life before you embark on the 'real thing'.

LIFE ABOARD 'THE QUEEN'

- In 30 years afloat, the *QE2* has sailed over four million sea miles.
- The passenger to staff ratio is two crew members for every three passengers.
- She has the largest floating library in the world.
- The on-board wine cellar holds 25,000 bottles of wine.
- During a cruise, 200 bottles of champagne are drunk every day.
- No other institution in the world orders more caviare each year.

SAILING SHIPS AND YACHTS and PASSENGER CARGO SHIPS

Main cruising regions

Company	US Lakes	Caribbean	Alaska	Mediterranean	Latin America	East Coast	North Europe	Indian Ocean	Far East	South Pacific	World
CAPTAIN COOK										•	
CLYDE OFFSHORE							•				•
COMP. DU PONANT		•		•							
DEILMANN		•		•							
DIRIGO		•			•	•				•	
GALILEO				•				•			
GREEK ISLANDS				•							
LEISURE CRUISES				•							
MAINE WINDJAMMER						•					
METROPOLITAN										•	
NAUTICAL RES.				•	•						
NORTH END						•					
OCEAN VOYAGES		•	•			•	•			•	
SEA CLOUD		•		•							
SONGLINES									•		
SQUARE SAIL PACIFIC										•	
STAR CLIPPERS		•		•					•		
TALL SHIP ADV.		•									
TRAVERSE	•										
VERMONT	•										
WHITSUNDAY ADV.										•	
WILDERNESS CH.										•	
WINDJAMMER B. FOOT		•									
WINDSTAR		•		•							
WORLDWIDE ADV.				•				•		•	
WORLDWIDE TRAVEL		•		•	•	•		•		•	
ZEUS		•		•							

Passenger Cargo Ships	US Lakes	Caribbean	Alaska	Mediterranean	Latin America	East Coast	North Europe	Indian Ocean	Far East	South Pacific	World
CO. POLYNÉSIENNE										•	
CURNOW							•	•			
IVARAN					•	•					
N.S.B.		•		•	•	•	•	•	•	•	•
POLISH OCEAN		•		•	•		•	•			

Useful Addresses

This section contains contact information for cruise lines and other organisations mentioned in the text. Note that in addition to their main office some of these companies may have various national and international sales offices, while others may be marketed internationally by other companies.

Telephone numbers in the USA and Canada with an '800' prefix are free when calling from within those countries. Calls from overseas are charged at international direct dialling rates.

AB Sea Cruises/Sailing School
131 Ernest St, Manly, Qld 4179, Australia.
tel: (+61) 07-3893-1240.

Abercrombie & Kent
1520 Kensington Rd, Oak Brook, IL 60521, USA.
Tel: (+1) 800-323-7309

Accessible Journeys
35 W. Sellers Ave, Ridley Park, PA 19078, USA.
Tel: (+1) 610-521-0339

African Safari Club
Urania Str. 40, Zürich, Switzerland.
Tel: (+41) 211-0870

Airtours Cruises
Wavell House, Holcombe Rd, Helmshore, Rossendale, Lancs BB4 4NB, UK.
tel: (+44) 01706-830130

Alaska Sightseeing/ Cruise West (AS/CW)
4th and Battery Building, Suite 700, Seattle, WA 98121, USA.
tel: (+1) 800-426-7702

Amazon Tours and Cruises
Reguena 336, Iquitos, Peru.
tel: (+51) 94-233-931

American Canadian Caribbean Line (ACCL)
461 Water St, PO Box 368, Warren, RI 02885, USA.
tel: (+1) 800-556-7450

American Hawaii Cruises
Two North Riverside Plaza, Chicago, IL 60606, USA.
tel: (+1) 800-765-7000
Web Site:http://www.cruise hawaii.com

American West Steamboat Company
520 Pike St, Suite 1400, Seattle, WA 98101, USA.
tel: (+1) 800-434-1232

Anytime Anywhere Travel
91 North Bedford Rd, Chappaqua, NY 10514, USA.
tel: (+1) 914-238-8800

Arcalia Shipping
Av. 24 de Julho, 126/128 - 53, 1300 Lisbon, Portugal.
tel: (+351) 1-395-3233

Australian Bareboat Charters
PO Box 357, Airlie Beach, Whitsunday, Qld 4802, Australia.
tel: (+61) 079-469-381
Web Site: http://www.ozemail.com.au/~bareboat

Awani Cruises
Artha Graha Tower, Jl Jend Sudirman Kav 52-53, Jakarta 12190, Indonesia.
tel: (+62) 021-515-2008

Bergen Line (Hurtigruten)
405 Park Ave, New York, NY 10022, USA.
tel: (+1) 800-666-2374

Berjaya Holiday Cruise
Plaza Berjaya Level 3, 12 Jalan Imbi, 55100 Kuala Lumpur, Malaysia.
tel: (+60) 3-245-5186

Black Sea Shipping (BLASCO)
ul. Lastochkina 1, 270026 Odessa, Ukraine.
tel: (+380) 48-7095-252160

Blakes Boating Holidays
Wroxham, Norwich, NR12 8DH, UK.
tel: (+44) 01603-782911

Blue Lagoon Cruises
Vitogo Parade, PO Box 130, Lautoka, Fiji Islands.
tel: (+679) 661-622

CDP Travel
5 Third St, Suite 820, San Francisco, California 94103, USA.
tel: (+1) 415-882-4490

Canaveral Cruise Line
751 Third Ave, New Smyrna Beach, FL 32169, USA.
tel: (+1) 904-427-6892

Captain Cook Cruises
No.6 Jetty, Circular Quay, Sydney NSW 2000, Australia.
tel: (+61) 02-9206-1122
Web Site: http://www.capt-cookcrus.com.au

Caravella Shipping
Lubyansky Proezd 25/1, 101000 Moscow, Russia.
tel: (+7) 095-924-2373

Cargo Ship Voyages
5 Hemley Hall Rd, Hemley, Woodbridge, Suffolk IP12 4QF, UK.
tel: (+44) 01473-736265

Carnival Cruise Lines
3655 NW 87th Avenue, Miami, FL 33178, USA.
tel: (+1) 800-327-9501
Web Site: http://www.carnival.com

Celebrity Cruises
5201 Blue Lagoon Drive, Miami, FL 33126, USA.
tel: (+1) 800-437-3111
Web Site:http://www.celebri-ty-cruises.com

China Yangtze River Shipping Company
89 Yanjiang Dadao, Hankou, Wuhan, Hubei Province 430000, China.
tel: (+86) 27-281-4543

Classical Cruises
132 East 70th St, New York, NY 10021, USA.
tel: (+1) 800-252-7745

Clipper Cruise Line
7711 Bonhomme Avenue, St Louis, MO 63105, USA.
tel: (+1) 800-325-0010

Clipper Cruiser Holidays
Akuna Bay, PO Box 180, Terrey Hills, NSW 2084, Australia.
tel: (+61) 02-9450-0000

Clyde Offshore Sailing Centre
Kip Marina, Inverkip, Renfrewshire PA16 OAS, Scotland, UK.
tel: (+44) 01475-521210

Commodore Cruise Line
4000 Hollywood Boulevard, South Tower, Suite 385, Hollywood, FL 33021, USA.
tel: (+1) 800-237-5361
WebSite: http://www.commodore.com

Compagnie des Isles du Ponant
60 Boulevard Marechal Juin, 44100 Nantes, France.
tel: (+33) 40-581495

Compagnie Polynésienne de Transport Maritime
B.P. 220, Papeete, Tahiti, French Polynesia.
tel: (+689) 426240

Coral Princess Cruises
Breakwater Terminal, Sir Leslie Thiess Drive, Townsville, Qld 4810, Australia.
tel: (+61) 77-211-673
Web Site: http://www.coral-princess.com.au

Costa Crociere
Via G d'Annuzi 5, Casa Postale 492, Genoa 16121, Italy.
tel: (+39) 10-54831

Costa Cruises
World Trade Center, 80 SW 8th St, Miami, FL 33130, USA.
tel: (+1) 800-462-6782
Web Site: http://www.costa.com

Cruceros Australis
Avenida El Bosque Norte 0440, Santiago, Chile.
tel: (+56) 2-203-5030

Cruise Company of Greenwich
31 Brookside Drive, Greenwich, CT 06830, USA.
tel: (+1) 800-825-0826

Cruise Lines International
1 Maritime Square #09-41, Singapore.
tel: (+65) 276-8682

Cruise People (The)
1252 Lawrence Avenue E. #202, Don Mills, Ontario M3A 1C3, Canada.
tel: (+1) 416-444-2410

Crystal Cruises
2121 Avenue of the Stars, Los Angeles, CA 90067, USA.
tel: (+1) 800-446-6620

Cunard Line
Suite 44, 610 Blue Lagoon Drive, Miami, Florida 33126, USA.
tel: (+1) 800-221-4770
Web Site: http://www.cunardline.com

Curnow Shipping
The Shipyard, Porthleven, Helston, Cornwall TR13 9JA, UK.
tel: (+44) 01326-563434

Deilmann Reederei (Peter Deilmann River & Ocean Cruises Ltd.)
Am Hafensteig 19, D-2430 Neustadt in Holstein, Germany.
tel: (+49) 4561-61060

Delphin Seereisen
Postfach 10 04 07 Offenbach/Main, 63004 Germany.
tel: (+49) 699-840-3811

Delta Queen Steamboat Company
Robin Street Wharf, 1380 Port of New Orleans Place, New Orleans, LA 70130, USA.
tel: (+1) 800-543-7637
Web Site: http://www.deltaqueen.com

Deutsche Seereederei,
PO Box 102188, 18003 Rostock, Germany.
tel: (+49) 0381-458-4097

Dirigo Cruises
39 Waterside Lane, Clinton, CT 06413, USA.
tel: (+1) 860-669-7068

Disney Cruise Line
210 Celebration Place, Suite 400, Celebration, FL 34747, USA.
tel: (+1) 407-939-3727
Web Site: http://www.disneycruise.com

Drifters Hotel Boats
PO Box 232, Worcester WR1 1BR, UK.
tel: (+44) 01905-610440

Empress Cruise Lines
C/o Berjaya Holiday Cruise, Plaza Berjaya Level 3, 12 Jalan Imbi, 55100 Kuala Lumpur, Malaysia.
tel: (+60) 3-245-5186

Equity Cruises
77–79 Great Eastern St, London EC2A 3HU, UK.
tel: (+44) 0171-729-1929

Esplanade Tours
581 Boylston St, Boston, MA 02116, USA.
tel: (+1) 800-426-5492

Eurocruises
303 West 13th St, New York, NY 10014, USA.
tel: (+1) 212-691-2099

Europe Cruise Line
Rijnkade 34, 6811 HA, Arnhem, Netherlands.
tel: (+31) 85-45-7611

European Waterways
Suite 404, Albany House, 324-326 Regent St, London W1R 5AA, UK.
tel: (+44) 0171-436-2931

Fantasy Cruises
5200 Blue Lagoon Drive, Miami, FL 33126, USA.
tel: (+1) 800-423-2100

Far Eastern Shipping Company (F.E.S.C.O.)
ul. Aleutskaya 15, 690019 Vladivostok, Russia.
tel: (+7) 4232-222432

Festival Cruises
99 Miaouli Akti, GR 185 38, Piraeus, Greece.
tel: (+30) 1-42-90769

Festive Cruises
Pate Court, North Place, Cheltenham, GL50 4DY, UK.
tel: (+44) 0990-553355

Flying Wheels Travel
143 W. Bridge St, Box 382, Owatonna, MN 55060, USA.
tel: (+1) 800-535-6790

Frachtschiff-Touristik (Capt. Peter Zylmann)
Exhöft 12, 24404 Maasholm, Germany
tel: (+49) 0-4642-6068

Fred Olsen Cruise Lines
Fred Olsen House, White House Rd, Ipswich, Suffolk IP1 5LL, UK.
tel: (+44) 01473-292200

Freighter Cruise Service
Suite 103, 5925 Monkland Ave, Montreal, Quebec H4A 1G7, Canada.
tel: (+1) 514-481-0447

Freighter World Cruises Inc.
180 South Lake Avenue, Suite 335, Pasadena, CA 91101, USA.
tel: (+1) 818-449-3106

French Country Waterways
PO Box 2195, Duxbury, MA 02331, USA.
tel: (+1) 800-222-1236

Galápagos Cruises
970 Ave. Republica de El Salvador, Box 17-12-0310, Quito, Ecuador.
tel: (+593) 2-464780

Galileo Cruises
Moutsopoulou Akti 58, Piraeus, 18536 Greece.
tel: (+30) 1-453-6405

Gdynia America Lines
Passenger Dept, 238 City Rd, London EC1V 2QL, UK.
tel: (+44) 0171-251-3389

Gill's Travel
23 Heol-Y-Deri, Rhiwbina, Cardiff CF4 6YF, Wales, UK.
tel: (+44) 01222-69-38-08

Glacier Bay Tours and Cruises
520 Pike St, Suite 1400, Seattle, WA 98101, USA.
tel: (+1) 800-451-5952

Golden Bear Travel
16 Digital Drive, Suite 100, Novato, CA 94948, USA.
tel: (+1) 800-551-1000

Golden Sun Cruises
71 Miaouli Akti, 185 37 Piraeus, Greece.
tel: (+30) 1-4512109

Göta Canal Steamship Company
PO Box 272, Hotellplatsen 2, Gothenburg, S-40124, Sweden.
tel: (+46) 031-806-315

Great Adventures
PO Box 898, Cairns, Qld 4870, Australia.
tel: (+61) 070-51-5644
Web Site: http://www.greatadventures.com.au

Greek Islands Cruise Center
50 Post Road West, Westport, Conn. 06880, USA.
tel: (+1) 800-341-3030

Grimaldi Cruises
Via C. D'Andrea, 80133 Naples, Italy.
tel: (+39) 81-551-7755

Hagen's Travel
320-1425 Marine Drive, West Vancouver, BC V7T 1B9, Canada.
tel: (+1) 604-926-4304

Hamburg-Süd Reiseagentur
Ost-West Str. 59-61, 20457 Hamburg, Germany.
tel: (+49) 040-3705-155

Hamburger Abendblatt/Die Welt
Verkaufsbüro/Seetouristik, Große Bleichen 68, 20354 Hamburg, Germany.
tel: (+49) 040-347-2-49-17

Hapag-Lloyd Cruises
Hapag Lloyd Haus, Ballindamm 25, D-20020 Hamburg, Germany.
tel: (+49) 040-30-010

Hebridean Island Cruises
Acorn Park, Skipton, N. Yorks BD23 2UE, UK.
tel: (+44) 01756-701380

Hilton International Nile Cruises
c/o Nile Hilton, PO Box 257, Cairo, Egypt.
tel: (+20) 5780-444

Holiday Inn/Asia Pacific
China Hong Kong City, 33 Canton Rd, Tower 3, 20/F, Kowloon, Hong Kong.
tel: (+852) 736-6955

Holland America Line
300 Elliott Avenue West, Seattle, WA 98119, USA.
tel: (+1) 800-426-0327
Web Site: http://www.hollandamerica.com

Hurtigruten
Troms Fylkes Dampskibsselskap, PO Box 548, 9001 Tromso, Norway.
tel: (+47) 083-86088

Inca Floats
1311 63rd St, Emeryville, CA 94608, USA.
tel: (+1) 510-420-1550

Intercruise
126 Kolokotroni St, 185 35 Piraeus, Greece.
tel: (+30) 1-42-83484

Irrawaddy Flotilla Company
Ancaster Business Centre, Cross St, Sterling, Scotland.
tel: (+44) 01877-382-998

Ivaran Lines
Vollsveien 9-11, PO Box 175, Lysaker, 1324 Oslo, Norway.
tel: (Norway) 02-539310

Jadrolinjia Cruises
Riva 16, 51000 Rijeka, Croatia.
tel: (+385) 51-30-899

Japan Cruise Line (Nippon Cruise Kyakusen)
Suite 5, 6th Floor, Nagaoka Building, 29-11 Hachobori 2-Chome, Chuo-Ku, Tokyo 104, Japan.
tel: (+81) 03-3555-1051

KD Deutsche Flusskreuzfahrten (KD River Cruises of Europe)
15 Frankenwerft, 50667 Köln, Germany.
tel: (+49) 0221-20880

Kangaroo Explorer
PO Box 7110, Cairns, Qld 4870, Australia.
tel: (+61) 70-324000
Web Site: http://www2.eis.net.au/-nqtds/infocomm/1pcr051.html

Kristina Cruises
Rannikolininjat OY, Korkeavouenkatu 2, SF-48100, Helsinki, Finland.
tel: (+358) 06-29968

Le Boat Inc.
PO Box E, Maywood, NJ 07607, USA.
tel: (+1) 800-922-0291

Le Cargo Club
Librairie Ulysse, 26 Rue Saint-Louis-en-l'Ile, 75004 Paris, France.
tel: (+33) 43-25-17-35

Leisure Cruises
Meienbergstrasse 80, PO Box 1312, CH-8645 Rapperswil-Jona, Switzerland.
tel: (+41) 55-220 84 00

Louis Cruise Lines
158 Franklin Roosevelt & Omonia Avenues, Limassol, Cyprus.
tel: (+357) 05-340000

Mabuhay Holiday Cruises
1008 10th Floor, City Land 10, Tower 2, Ayala Avenue, Corner de la Costa St, Makati City, Manila, Philippines.
tel: (+63) 2-893-2211

Maine Windjammer Association
Box 137, Rockport, ME 04856, USA.
tel: (+1) 207-594-8007

Mar Line
Hoteles Marinos, Edificio Hoteles Playa, Carrera Faro Sabinal S/N, 04740 Roquetas de Mar, Almeira, Spain.
tel: n/a

Marine Expeditions
13 Hazelton Avenue, Toronto, Ontario M5R 2E1, Canada.
tel: (+1) 800-263-9147

Mediterranean Shipping Cruises (MSC)
Piazza Garibaldi 91, 80142 Napoli, Italy.
tel: (+39) 81-554-54-11

Mer et Voyages
3 Rue Tronchet, 75008 Paris, France
tel: (+33) 1-44-51-01-68

Metro Holdings
391B Orchard Rd, 23-01 Tower B, Ngee Ann City, 238874 Singapore.
tel: (+65) 739-9866

Metropolitan Touring
13150 Coit Rd, Suite 10, Dallas, TX 75240, USA.
tel: (+1) 800-527-2500

Mirimar Cruises
Queens Wharf Rd, North Quay, PO Box 12251, Elizabeth St, Brisbane 4002, Australia.
tel: (+61) 07-3221-0300

Mitsui O.S.K Passenger Line
Shosen Mitsui Bldg, 1 Toranomon, 2-Chrome, Minato-Ku, Tokyo 105, Japan.
tel: (+81) 03-3587-7111

Murmansk Shipping
ul. Kominterna 15, 183636 Murmansk, Russia.
tel: (+7) 8152-522451

N.S.B. (Niederelbe Schiffahrtsgesellschaft) Frachtschiff-Touristik
Violenstr. 22, D-28195 Bremen, Germany.
tel: (+49) 0421-321668

NYK (Nippon Yusen Kaisha) Cruises
3-2 Marunouchi 2-Chome, Chiyoda-Ku, Tokyo 100, Japan.
tel: (+81) 03-3284-6001

Nabila Nile Cruises
605 Market St, Suite 1310, San Francisco, CA 94105, USA.
tel: (+1) 415-979-0160

Nautical Resources, Inc.
666 Fifth Avenue, New York, NY 10103, USA.
tel: (+1) 800-398-6244.

Neckermann Seereisen
Zimmersmuehlenweg 55, 61440 Oberursel, Germany.
tel: (+49) 6172-92520

New Century Cruise Lines
100 Orchard Rd, #02-01, Singapore.
tel: (+65) 732-6765

Nina Cruise Line,
Via T Galimberti 7/2, 16128 Genoa, Italy.
tel: (+39) 10-588911

Niugini Cruises
PO Box 371, Mount Hagen, Western Province, Papua New Guinea.
tel: (+675) 521438

Noble Caledonia
11 Charles St, Mayfair, London W1X 8LE, UK.
tel: (+44) 0171-409-0376

North End Shipyard Schooners
P.O. Box 482, Rockland, Maine 04841, USA.
tel: (+1) 207-594-8007
Web Site: http://www.midcoast.com/-schooner

Norwegian Cruise Line (NCL)
95 Merrick Way, Coral Gables, FL 33134, USA.
tel: (+1) 800-327-7030
Web Site: http://www.ncl.com

Oberoi Nile Cruises
Mena House Oberoi, Pyramids Rd, Giza, Cairo, Egypt.
tel: (+20) 2-383-3222

Ocean Voyages
1709 Bridgeway, Sausalito, CA 94965, USA.
tel: (+1) 415-332-4681

OdessAmerica Cruise Company
170 Old Country Rd, Suite 608, Mineola, NY 11501, USA.
tel: (+1) 800-221-3254

Olivia Cruises
4400 Market St, Oakland, CA 94608, USA.
tel: (+1) 510-655-0364

Orient Lines
38 Park St, London W1Y 3PF, UK.
tel: (+44) 0171-409-2500

P & O Cruises
77 New Oxford St, London WC1A 1PP, UK.
tel: (+44) 0171-800-2222

Page & Moy Ltd.
136–140 London Rd, Leicester LE2 1EN, UK.
tel: (+44) 01942-526121

Paradise Cruises
52 Kitiou Kyprianou St, PO Box 157, Limassol, Cyprus.
tel: (+357) 05-369000

Paul Mundy Cruising
5/7 Quadrant Arcade, Regent St, London W1R 6JB, UK.
tel: (+44) 0171-734-4404

Pearl's Travel Tips
9903 Oaks Lane, Seminole, FL 34642, USA.
tel: (+1) 813-393-2919

Phoenix Reisen
Kölnstraße 80, D-53111 Bonn, Germany.
tel: (+49) 0228-72-62-855

Polish Ocean Lines
POL Passenger Department, Dluga 76, 80-831 Gdansk, Poland.
tel: (+48) 58-314851

Premier Cruises
400 Challenger Rd, Cape Canaveral, FL 32920, USA
tel: (+1) 407-783-5061

Presidential Nile Cruises
13 Maraashli Str, Zamalek, Cairo, Egypt.
tel: (+20) 2-3400517

Princess Cruises
10100 Santa Monica Blvd, Los Angeles, CA 90067, USA.
tel: (+1) 310-553-1770
Web Site: http://www.princesscruises.com

Proud Australia Holidays
Level 2, Stafford House, 23 Leigh St, Adelaide SA 5000, Australia.
tel: (+61) 8-8231-9472

Pure Pleasure Cruises
PO Box 1831, Townsville, 4810 North Qld, Australia.
tel: (+61) 077-213555

Quark Expeditions
980 Post Rd, Darien, CT 06820, USA.
tel: (+1) 800-356-5699
Web Site: http://www.quark-expeditions.com

Quicksilver Connections
Marina Mirage, Port Douglas, Qld. 4871, Australia.
tel: (+61) 070-99-5500
Web Site: http://www.ozemail.co.au/~quick3

R.S.V.P. Cruises
2800 University Avenue Southeast, Minneapolis, MN 55414, USA.
tel: (+1) 612-379-4697

Radisson Seven Seas Cruises,
600 Corporate Drive, Suite 410, Fort Lauderdale, FL33334, USA.
tel: (+1) 800-333-3333
Web Site: http://www.ten-io.com/radisson/

Regal Cruises
4199 34th St, Suite B103, St Petersburg, FL 33711, USA.
tel: (+1) 813-867-1300

Regal China Cruises
4F, No. 2, Pa Teh Rd, Sec 3 Taipei, Taiwan.
tel: (+886) 2-557-1528

Renaissance Cruises
1800 Eller Drive, Suite 300, Ft. Lauderdale, FL 33335, USA.
tel: (+1) 800-525-5350
Web Site: http://www.rencruises.com

Royal Caribbean International
1050 Caribbean Way, Miami, FL 33132, USA.
tel: (+1) 800-327-6700
Web Site: http://www.royal-caribbean.com

Royal Hispania Cruises (Royal Hispania Cruceros)
Paso de la Castillana, Torre Europa - Planta 26, 28046 Madrid, Spain.
tel: (+34) 91-555-1311

Royal Olympic Cruises
87 Miaouli Akti, 185 38 Piraeus, Greece.
tel: (+30) 1-42-91000

Royal Seas Cruise Line
507 North Florida Ave, Tampa, FL 33602, USA.
tel: (+1) 800-290-6222

Roylen Cruises
PO Box 169, Mackay, Qld 4740, Australia.
tel: (+61) 7-49-553066
Web Site: http://www.roylen.com.au

St. Lawrence Cruise Lines
253 Ontario St, Kingston, Ontario K7L 2Z4, Canada.
tel: (+1) 800-267-7868

Saga Holidays
The Saga Building, Middleburg Square, Folkestone, Kent CT20 1AZ, UK.
tel: (+44) 0800-50 50 30

Sea Cloud Cruises
Vorstzen 50, D-20459 Hamburg, Germany.
tel: (+49) 40-369-0272

Sea the Difference Inc.
420 Fifth Ave, New York, NY 10018, USA.
tel: (+1) 212-354-4409

Seabourn Cruise Line
55 Francisco St, San Francisco, CA 94133, USA.
tel: (+1) 800-929-4747

Seetours International
Seilerstrasse 23, 60313 Frankfurt, Germany.
tel: (+49) 691-3330.

SeniorTours
508 Irvington Rd, Drexel Hill, PA 19026, USA.
tel: (+1) 215-626-1977

Sheraton Nile Cruises
Ahmed Pacha St. 4, Garden City, Cairo, Egypt.
tel: (+20) 2-355-6664

Siam Cruise Company
Chaiyod Arcade, 33/10-11, Sukhumvit Soi 11 Rd, Klongtoey, Phrakanong, Bangkok 10110, Thailand.
tel: (+66) 2-255-8950

Silversea Cruises
110 East Broward Blvd, Ft. Lauderdale, FL 33301, USA.
tel: (+1) 800-722-9055

Singleworld
401 Theodore Fremd Ave, Rye, NY 10580, USA.
tel: (+1) 800-223-6490

Society Expeditions
2001 Western Avenue, Suite 710, Seattle, WA 98121, USA.
tel: (+1) 800-548-8669

SongLines Cruises
Jalan Kenanga II/2, Jaka Permai Bekasi, Jakarta 17145, Indonesia.
tel: (+62) 21-8842218

Sonnesta Hotels
4 El Tayaran St, Nasr City, Cairo, Egypt.
tel: (+20) 2-262-8111

Southern Heritage Expeditions
6033 West Century Boulevard, No. 1270, Los Angeles, CA 90045, USA.
tel: (+1) 800-351-2323

Special Expeditions
123 South Avenue East, 3rd Floor, Westfield, NJ 07090, USA.
tel: (+1) 800-348-2358

Spice Island Cruises
Jalan Padang Galak No. 134, Sanur, Denpasar 80227, Bali, Indonesia.
tel: (+62) 0361-286-283

Square Sail Pacific
PO Box 32247, Devpt, Auckland, New Zealand.
tel: (+64) 9-413-8644

Star Clippers
4101 Salzedo Ave, Coral Gables, FL 33146, USA.
tel: (+1) 800-442-0551

Star Cruise
391B Orchard Rd, 13-01 Ngee Ann City, Tower B, Singapore 0923.
tel: (+65) 733-6388

Strand Voyages
Charing Cross Shopping Concourse, The Strand, London WC2N 4HZ, UK.
tel: (+44) 0171-836-6363

Svalbard Polar Travel
PO Box 540, Longyearbyen, 9170 Norway.
tel: (+1) 790-21-971

Swan Hellenic Cruises
77 New Oxford St, London WC1A 1PP, UK.
tel: (+44) 0171-800-2200

TT-Line Company
Station Pier PO Box 323, Port Melbourne, Victoria 3207, Australia.
tel: (+61) 13-20-10
Web Site: http://www.tt-line.com.au

Tall Ship Adventures
1389 South Havana St, Aurora, CO 80012, USA.
tel: (+1) 800-662-0090

Temptress Cruises
1600 Northwest LeJeune Rd, Suite 301, Miami, FL 33126, USA.
tel: (+1) 800-336-8423

Thomson Cruises
Greater London House, Hampstead Rd, London NW1 7SD, UK.
tel: (+44) 0171-707-9000

Transocean Reederei
Palmaille 45, Postfach 501522, 22767 Hamburg, Germany.
tel: (+49) 40-380160

Travel Companion Exchange
PO Box 833, Amityville, NY 11701, USA.
tel: (+1) 800-392-1256

Traverse Tall Ship Company
13390 W. Bay Shore Drive, Traverse City, Michigan 49684, USA.
tel: (+1) 800-678-0383

TravLtips
163-07 Depot Rd, PO Box 188, Flushing, NY 11358, USA.
tel: (+1) 718-939-2400

UK Waterway Holidays
1 Port Hill, Hertford, SG14 1P, UK.
tel: (+44) 01992-550616

Venice Simplon Orient Express (V.S.O.E.) Cruises
Sea Containers House, 20 Upper Ground, London SE1 9PF, UK.
tel: (+44) 0171-805-5060

Vergina Cruises
271 Alkiviadou St, 185 36 Piraeus, Greece.
tel: (+30) 1-428-5803

Vermont Schooner Cruises
Box 800, Bristol, Vermont 05443, USA.
tel: (+1) 802-453-4818

Victoria Cruises
57-08 39th Avenue Woodside, New York, NY 11377, USA.
tel: (+1) 800-348-8084

Voyages of Discovery
Première House, Betts Way, Crawley RH10 2GB, UK.
tel: (+44) 01293-433030

Voyages Jules Verne
21 Dorset Square, London NW1 6QG, UK.
tel: (+44) 0171-616-1000
Web Site: http://www.vjv.co.uk

Wagner Frachtschiffreisen
Stradlerstr. 48, CH-8404 Winterthur, Switzerland.
tel: (+41) 052-242-1442

Waverley Excursions Ltd.
Anderston Quay, Glasgow G3 8HA, Scotland, UK.
tel: (+44) 0141-221-8152

Whitsunday Adventure Sailing
PO Box 519, Airlie Beach, Queensland 4802, Australia.
tel: (+61) 079-461-777
Web Site: http://www.whitsunday.net.au

Whitsunday Escape
PO Box 719, Airlie Beach, Qld 4802, Australia.
tel: (+61) 079-465-222

Wilderness Challenge
PO Box 254, Cairns, Qld 4870, Australia.
tel: (+61) 070-55-6504
Web Site: http://www.ozemail.com.au/~wildchal

Wilderness Travel
801 Allston Way, Berkeley, CA 94710, USA.
tel: (+1) 800-368-2794

Windjammer Barefoot Cruises
1759 Bay Rd, Miami Beach, Florida, FL 33139, USA.
tel: (+1) 800-327-2602
Web Site: http://www.windjammer.com

Windstar Cruises
300 Elliott Avenue West, Seattle, WA 98119, USA.
tel: (+1) 800-258-7245
Web Site: http://www.windstar-cruises.com

World Explorer Cruises
555 Montgomery St, San Francisco, CA 94111, USA.
tel: (+1) 800-854-3835

Worldwide Adventures
36 Finch Ave. West, North York, Ontario M2N 2G9, Canada.
tel: (+1) 800-387-1483

Worldwide Travel & Cruise Associates
400 SE 12th St, Fort Lauderdale, FL 33316, USA.
tel: (+1) 800-881-8484

Zeus Cruises
566 Seventh Avenue, New York, NY 10018, USA.
tel: (+1) 800-447-5667

INDEX

Page numbers in **bold** refer to captions accompanying illustrations